A follow-up to **Becoming a Millionaire:** *Rules of Engagement for Beginners*

100 BUSINESSES
Anyone Can Do To Make & Grow Wealth

A Compendium of Business Templates for a Typical Developing Economy

BEBRA WISDOM PERELAH

A follow-up to **Becoming a Millionaire:** *Rules of Engagement for Beginners*

100 BUSINESSES
Anyone Can Do To Make & Grow Wealth

A Compendium of Business Templates for a Typical Developing Economy

BEBRA WISDOM PERELAH

100 Businesses Anyone Can Do To Make & Grow Wealth
A Compendium of Business Templates for a Typical Developing Economy

ISBN: 978-978-765-068-4

Published and printed by:

Pen-Impact Writing and Publishing Enterprise
16 Adedoyin Rhodes-Vivour Close, Asokoro,
Abuja, FCT, Nigeria
Website: www.pen-impact.com
Email: info@pen-impact.com
Tel: +234 701 990 4999

Dedication

This book is dedicated to every young person who was not born with a silver spoon in his/her mouth and is doing everything to change the story in this lifetime.

Acknowledgement

I want to deeply express my appreciation to my friends, who wouldn't let me give up on putting these ideas together. They believed in me and never stopped saying it until this book was completed.

Introduction

Economic realities in third-world countries have been hostile and volatile in recent times. This calls for desperate measures, insane ideas, an out-of-the-book approach and a timely intervention customised to suit our environment. Systems established by various governments do not work to support the survival of enterprises; they would rather kill the available ones. Some of the most reliable, resilient and formidable companies are leaving Nigeria, and this is an indicator of an economic drought. It is pertinent to note at this juncture that Nigerian businesses must now be structured with adaptive measures to insulate against the effects of the stormy economy.

Though these are trying times for the lovely people of Nigeria, they come with opportunities that will strengthen entrepreneurs to build businesses that will outlast any storm and, in the end, culminate into some of the strongest business prototypes for the future business world to come and study. As entrepreneurs, our minds are modified to see opportunities in any problem, and Nigeria is full of opportunities and untapped potentials. The Nigerian business terrain is like a virgin land, and its fertility cannot be overemphasised.

Certain companies have already seen the instability and have evolved to meet the ever-changing demands. Some companies knew a long time ago that a time like this would come, so they had diversified appropriately into other areas of the economy. Due to the economy's instability, some mono-product companies have delved into producing other products. Those who were resistant to these drastic economic changes have suffered great externalities.

Successive governments have failed to directly address the economic abyss in this country as they continue with the mantra of providing jobs for people. Governments in saner climes enable the private sector to create jobs by providing the necessary facilities, special tax regimes, credit facilities, security of business environments, prioritisation of business interests, and provision of requisite infrastructure to enhance the survival of businesses, which will, in turn, employ the teaming population of young people out there.

However, Nigerians who are bound to Nigeria are left with no option but to seek self-help. There are innumerable needs in Nigeria, and businesses/enterprises must be formed to cater for those needs and make money for the owners and those who work for them; hence, the importance of this book. The book is a continuation of another book, *Becoming A Millionaire: Rules of Engagement for Beginners.*

This book aims to provide workable business templates for a typical Nigerian and sub-Saharan economy. It will provide sketches of one hundred businesses that can meet people's needs and activate cash flow for their owners.

Disclaimer

This book is a compendium of business templates, and prospective readers are advised to do due diligence on whichever templates they choose to adopt. The failure of any such businesses is not the burden of this book, and the book is not liable for your mismanagement and misjudgment. Business decisions are your personal decisions, and this book is only a guide to your selection process.

This book does not and will not take responsibility for any failure in your business or any other type of investment. It only provides sample businesses that could form the skeletal framework of your new enterprise or guide you in decision-making.

Why This Book?

My interactions with men of different pedigrees revealed that most of them would love to be financially independent and stable, but they do not know how. Some are stagnated by generational habits; others simply misplace priorities, and others are impeded by ignorance. This book will give insight into what you can do to help yourself apart from your paid job with the government or a company. The book will be precise in its attempt to paint a picture to help the reader understand the right thing to do.

Sources Of Business

The most reliable source of business is problems. Entrepreneurs are not just looking for money at all costs; they provide solutions to specific problems and make money for themselves. When I say business, it could be a service-based business or a product-based business, but either way, its continued effectiveness is dependent on whether or not it solves a problem and how prevalent such problems are.

The first factor to consider when sourcing for a business is **the environment.** The environmental factor dictates the actual type of business you should venture into, and this is the reason why it is difficult to give a definitive answer when I am asked, "*What kind of business can I do*?" The problems, needs and wants of the people are relative to the environment, and as such, people attempting to venture into business for the first time must gather their data from the environment. Most suburban environments lack so many things, thereby creating room for business. Having learned this, I shall go on to provide brief highlights on different kinds of businesses anyone can select from in order to make decisions. This book will not go into detail on any of the business concepts that will be suggested, as it is expected that readers who want to swing into action will pick one that provides a solution to a known problem in their environment and research further into the specifics of such business templates before they establish such business.

100 Business Templates for Nigerians and Other Developing Economies

1. POULTRY FARMING

It is worrisome to think that poultry products are still being imported into this country at this age and time. Another indicator of this trend is that there is a huge demand for chicken, eggs, and related products in Nigeria. This is why the people in this line of business are making good money. Though this line of business has its own risks, if we're prepared for them, they could bring lifetime financial assistance to individuals or families.

2. FISH FARMING

Nigeria is a blessed country because of its population, which makes the demand for fish high. Despite the fact that thousands of tons of foreign frozen fish are imported into the country, the consumption of locally farmed fish like catfish is on the high side. Farmed catfish can be seen as the major stock available even in local riverine markets, which are areas considered to be inhabited by traditional fishermen.

People living in coastal areas could farm fish more profitably, while freshwater regions could utilise floating ponds in the rivers, thereby avoiding the cost of pumping water daily.

3. SNAIL FARMING

Snail farming in Nigeria involves breeding and raising snails for commercial purposes. It requires suitable climate and soil conditions. Farmers typically provide proper housing, feed, and management to ensure optimal growth. The Achatina species is commonly farmed. Snail farming offers a potential income source due to the growing demand for snails in local and international markets.

4. CATTLE FARMING

Cattle farming in Nigeria as a business involves raising cattle for various purposes, such as meat production, milk, and leather. Farmers need suitable land, proper housing, and nutritional management for the cattle. Breeds like Fulani, Sokoto Gudali, and Red Bororo are common. It's crucial to consider health care, vaccinations, and disease prevention. Cattle farming can be profitable through the sale of meat and other by-products, contributing to the agricultural economy in Nigeria.

5. GOAT FARMING

Goat farming involves breeding and raising goats for meat, milk, fibre, and other products. In Nigeria, goat farming has promising prospects due to several factors. Goats are hardy, adaptable to diverse climates, and have a relatively short gestation period, allowing for quick returns. Popular breeds include the Boer, Nubian, and Saanen.

Prospects for goat farming in Nigeria include:

1. *Meat Production*: Goat meat is widely consumed, and there is a consistent demand for it, making goat farming a lucrative venture.
2. *Milk Production:* Certain goat breeds, like the Saanen and Alpine, are known for high milk yields. Goat milk is nutritious and has a growing market.
3. *Fibre Production:* Angora and Cashmere goats can provide high-quality fibres for textiles, adding another dimension to the business.
4. *Manure:* Goat manure is a valuable organic fertilizer that contributes to sustainable farming practices.
5. *Disease Resistance:* Goats are generally hardy and resilient, making them suitable for various agroecological zones in Nigeria.
6. *Small-Scale Farming:* Goat farming is adaptable to small-scale operations, allowing farmers with limited resources to participate.

To succeed, goat farmers should focus on proper nutrition, disease prevention, and good management practices. Additionally, exploring value-added products like cheese and soap can enhance profitability. Overall, goat farming presents a viable and sustainable agribusiness opportunity in Nigeria.

6. PIG FARMING

Pig farming, or pig rearing, in Nigeria, can be a lucrative business venture with various prospects. Here's a brief overview:

1. *Meat Production:* Pork is a popular meat choice, and there is a consistent demand for it in Nigeria. Pig farming allows for efficient meat production.

2. *Reproduction Rate:* Pigs have a high reproductive rate, with sows capable of producing large litters, leading to quick turnover and potential profits.
3. *Feed Conversion:* Pigs efficiently convert feed into meat, making them a cost-effective option for meat production.
4. *Manure:* Pig manure is rich in nutrients and can be used as fertilizer, providing an additional income stream or contributing to crop farming.
5. *Adaptability:* Pigs can adapt to different environmental conditions and can be raised on a small or large scale.
6. *Value-Added Products:* Besides meat, there's potential for producing value-added products such as sausages, bacon, and other processed pork items.

Success in pig farming in Nigeria requires attention to factors like proper housing, nutrition, disease control, and breeding management. Farmers should also consider biosecurity measures to prevent diseases. As with any business, understanding market demand, effective marketing strategies, and financial management are crucial for long-term success in pig farming.

7. RABBIT FARMING

Rabbit rearing as a business involves breeding and raising rabbits for various purposes, such as meat, fur, and pet trade. In Nigeria, rabbit farming is gaining popularity due to its several advantages;

1. *High Reproductive Rate*: Rabbits reproduce quickly, leading to a rapid increase in population and potential for high production.

2. *Meat Production*: Rabbit meat is low in fat and cholesterol, making it a healthy alternative. There's a growing market demand for rabbit meat.

3. *Low Space Requirements:* Rabbits can be raised in relatively small spaces, making them suitable for urban and peri-urban areas.

4. *Quick Turnover*: Rabbits mature quickly, allowing for a faster return on investment compared to some larger livestock.

5. *Manure*: Rabbit droppings are rich in nutrients and can be used as an excellent organic fertilizer.

6. *Dual-Purpose Breeds*: Some rabbit breeds are versatile, providing both meat and fur, adding to the potential income streams.

Proper housing, nutrition, and disease management are crucial for rabbit farming success. Farmers should also consider marketing strategies to tap into the demand for rabbit products. Overall, rabbit rearing offers a viable and sustainable agribusiness option, especially for those with limited space and resources.

8. TURKEY FARMING

Turkey farming as a household business in Nigeria presents a viable opportunity for individuals looking to engage in poultry production. Turkeys are primarily raised for meat, and their fast growth rate makes them suitable for a relatively short production cycle. This aspect is particularly advantageous for households seeking a quick return on investment. The adaptability of turkeys to different environmental conditions makes them well-suited for various regions in Nigeria, providing flexibility for small-scale operations.

Furthermore, turkey farming offers dual-purpose benefits as certain breeds can provide both meat and eggs. This diversification can contribute to a more stable income for households. Additionally, during festive seasons, there tends to be an increased demand for turkey meat, presenting marketing opportunities for local producers. Success in turkey farming at the household level requires attention to proper housing, nutrition, and disease prevention. By tapping into the market demand and implementing sound management practices, households can establish a sustainable and profitable venture with turkey farming in Nigeria.

9. GRASSCUTTER FARMING

Grasscutter farming, also known as cane rat farming, is gaining traction as a viable business in developing countries due to several factors. These rodents are native to Africa and are known for their high reproductive rate, making them prolific breeders. In countries like Nigeria, grasscutter farming is seen as a sustainable source of protein and income. Grasscutters are appreciated for their lean meat, which is considered a healthy alternative. Their ability to thrive in various climates and adapt to different environments contributes to the suitability of grasscutter farming in developing countries.

The grasscutter farming business also aligns well with small-scale operations commonly found in developing regions. Grasscutters can be reared in limited spaces and fed on a variety of locally available vegetation, reducing the dependency on costly feeds. Additionally, their quick maturity and high reproductive rate lead to a fast turnover, enabling farmers to see returns on investment relatively quickly. This aspect is crucial for individuals with limited resources seeking sustainable agribusiness opportunities in developing countries.

However, success in grasscutter farming requires proper knowledge of their behaviour, nutritional needs, and suitable housing. Disease management and biosecurity measures are also vital to ensure a healthy and productive grasscutter population. Developing effective marketing strategies and tapping into local demand for grasscutter meat can further enhance the economic viability of this farming venture. Overall, grasscutter farming stands out as a promising agribusiness in developing countries, offering both nutritional benefits and economic opportunities for local communities.

10. CROP FARMING (e.g., maize, cassava, vegetables)

Crop farming in Nigeria, encompassing crops like maize, cassava, and various vegetables, is a crucial component of the country's agricultural landscape and presents a viable business opportunity. Maize, a staple food, is in high demand for both human consumption and livestock feed. Its versatility extends to industrial applications, making it a versatile and profitable crop. Cassava, another staple, is a drought-resistant and high-yielding crop, contributing significantly to food security and income generation. With its diverse uses in food processing and as a raw material for various industries, cassava farming has economic importance beyond the household level.

Vegetable farming, including crops like tomatoes, peppers, and leafy greens, plays a pivotal role in meeting the nutritional needs of the population. The growing urbanisation and increasing awareness of healthy diets contribute to the rising demand for fresh vegetables. Entrepreneurs engaging in vegetable farming can benefit from this demand while contributing to food diversity and nutrition. Additionally, vegetable farming allows for small-scale operations, making it accessible to individuals with limited resources. The accessibility of markets, both local and international, provides avenues for farmers to expand their business and contribute to the agricultural economy.

Success in crop farming as a business in Nigeria requires careful consideration of factors such as soil health, water management, and pest control. Sustainable and organic farming practices are gaining importance as consumers become more conscious of food quality. Adopting modern agricultural technologies, accessing credit facilities, and participating in farmer cooperatives can enhance the productivity and profitability of crop farming ventures. Furthermore, continuous education on innovative farming techniques and market trends can empower farmers to make informed decisions, contributing to the growth and sustainability of crop farming businesses in Nigeria.

11. PLANTAIN CULTIVATION

Plantain and its by-products play a significant role in the Nigerian economy, contributing to both food security and economic growth. Plantain is a staple crop widely consumed across the country, providing a crucial source of carbohydrates, vitamins, and minerals. Its popularity in local diets makes it an essential component of food security initiatives, addressing the nutritional needs of the population.

Beyond direct consumption, plantain has economic importance through various by-products. Plantain farming generates income and employment opportunities for many Nigerians. Farmers engage in the cultivation, harvesting, and sale of plantains, contributing to the agricultural sector's growth. The processing of plantain into by-products, such as plantain flour and plantain chips, further expands its economic impact. Plantain flour, commonly known as *"elubo"* or "*amala*," is a versatile ingredient used in traditional Nigerian dishes. The production and sale of plantain flour create entrepreneurship opportunities and support small-scale agribusinesses, fostering economic development at the grassroots level.

Additionally, plantain chips have become a popular snack, both domestically and internationally. The commercialisation of plantain chips provides avenues for export, contributing to foreign exchange earnings. This diversification of plantain products not only boosts the income of farmers and processors but also enhances the country's economic resilience by tapping into different markets.

In summary, plantain and its by-products play a dual role in the Nigerian economy by addressing food security concerns and creating economic opportunities. The crop's versatility, from direct consumption to various processed forms, underscores its significance in sustaining livelihoods and contributing to the overall economic development of Nigeria.

12. BEEKEEPING

Beekeeping, or apiculture, is a business that is often underestimated in developing countries despite its tremendous potential for economic growth, environmental sustainability, and poverty alleviation. In many developing regions, beekeeping is traditionally viewed as a subsistence activity rather than a thriving business. However, its impact goes beyond producing honey, extending to various valuable by-products and ecosystem services.

One of the leading products of beekeeping is honey, a natural sweetener in high demand both locally and internationally. Beekeeping provides a source of income for small-scale farmers and entrepreneurs. In addition to honey, other bee-related products like beeswax, royal jelly, and propolis have various applications in cosmetics, medicine, and industry. These by-products can contribute significantly to the revenue generated from beekeeping operations.

Moreover, beekeeping enhances environmental sustainability by promoting pollination, a critical process for agriculture. Many crops depend on pollinators like bees to reproduce, and increased bee populations can boost agricultural productivity. Beekeeping businesses, therefore, indirectly support food production and food security in developing countries

13. GREENHOUSE FARMING

Greenhouse farming as a business in Nigeria presents a promising venture with several advantages, offering solutions to challenges faced by traditional open-field agriculture. Here's a detailed discussion:

1. *Year-Round Production:* Greenhouse farming allows for year-round cultivation, overcoming seasonal limitations. In Nigeria, where weather patterns can be unpredictable, greenhouses provide a controlled environment, enabling continuous production and consistent crop yields.
2. *Crop Diversification:* Greenhouses support the cultivation of a wide variety of crops, from vegetables to flowers. This diversification allows farmers to respond to market demands and grow high-value crops that might be challenging in open fields.
3. *High-Quality Produce:* The controlled environment in greenhouses ensures optimal conditions for crop growth. This results in high-quality produce that meets market standards, leading to better pricing and increased marketability. The demand for premium-quality fruits

and vegetables is growing in both local and international markets.

4. *Resource Efficiency:* Greenhouse technologies, such as drip irrigation and precision farming, optimise the use of water, fertilizers, and pesticides. This not only reduces resource waste but also contributes to sustainable agricultural practices, addressing concerns like water scarcity and environmental impact.

5. *Crop Protection:* Greenhouses act as a barrier against pests and diseases, minimising the need for chemical pesticides. This not only enhances food safety but also aligns with the increasing consumer preference for organic and pesticide-free produce.

6. *Job Creation:* Greenhouse farming requires specialised skills in crop management, climate control, and technology utilisation. As the sector expands, it contributes to job creation, especially in rural areas. Training programmes and capacity-building initiatives can further enhance skill development within the workforce.

7. *Climate Resilience:* Greenhouses provide a level of climate resilience by shielding crops from extreme weather conditions. In a country like Nigeria, which is susceptible to weather fluctuations and climate change effects, resilience is crucial for stable and reliable agricultural production.

8. *Economic viability:* While initial setup costs for greenhouses can be relatively high, the long-term economic benefits often outweigh the investment. Increased yields, better-quality produce, and access to niche markets contribute to the economic viability of greenhouse farming as a business in Nigeria.

9. *Access to Finance and Support:* To promote greenhouse farming, access to financing and government support programmes are essential. Initiatives providing subsidised loans, technical assistance, and infrastructure development can encourage more farmers to adopt greenhouse technology.

In conclusion, greenhouse farming in Nigeria presents a dynamic and profitable business opportunity, offering solutions to challenges faced by traditional agriculture. As technology advances and awareness grows, the adoption of greenhouse farming is likely to increase, contributing to the modernisation and sustainability of Nigeria's agricultural sector.

14. HERB FARMING

Herb farming is indeed a profitable business with numerous advantages. The increasing global demand for fresh, organic herbs has created a lucrative market for herb farmers. Herbs are sought after not only for culinary purposes but also for medicinal and cosmetic uses, contributing to their versatility and high market value. Entrepreneurs in herb farming can cultivate a diverse range of herbs, such as basil, mint, rosemary, and lavender, catering to various industries and consumer preferences.

One key factor contributing to the profitability of herb farming is the relatively low input costs compared to some other crops. Herbs often require less space, water, and fertilizer, making them a cost-effective option for farmers. Additionally, many herbs have high growth rates and can be harvested multiple times in a year, providing a quicker return on investment. The ability to diversify products, such as selling fresh herbs and dried herbs or even creating value-added products like herbal teas or essential oils, further enhances the revenue streams for herb farmers. The rising interest in healthy lifestyles and natural remedies adds to the demand for herbs, making herb farming a sustainable and profitable venture for those who choose to enter this agribusiness.

15. MUSHROOM FARMING

Mushroom farming in Nigeria is emerging as a viable and profitable agribusiness, offering several advantages to entrepreneurs and contributing to the diversification of the agricultural sector. One key benefit of mushroom farming is its ability to thrive in various environmental conditions and limited space, making it accessible to both rural and urban farmers. Common varieties cultivated in Nigeria include oyster mushrooms, shiitake, and white button mushrooms.

The demand for mushrooms in Nigeria has been on the rise due to their nutritional value, distinct flavours, and versatility in culinary applications. Mushrooms are rich in protein, vitamins, and minerals, appealing to health-conscious consumers. As a result, mushroom farming provides an opportunity for farmers to tap into a growing market and diversify their agricultural activities. Moreover, mushrooms can be cultivated using agricultural waste products, such as rice straw or sawdust, contributing to sustainable farming practices and waste utilisation.

Mushroom farming also holds the potential for quick returns on investment. Depending on the mushroom variety, cultivation cycles are relatively short, allowing farmers to harvest multiple times in a year. This rapid turnover, combined with the increasing demand for mushrooms, makes it an attractive business proposition. Entrepreneurs can explore various products, including fresh mushrooms, dried mushrooms, and value-added products like mushroom powder or extracts, thereby expanding their market reach and revenue streams.

However, successful mushroom farming requires careful attention to hygiene, temperature, and humidity control, as well as proper substrate preparation. Farmers can benefit from training programmes and support from agricultural extension services to enhance their knowledge and skills in mushroom cultivation. Overall, mushroom farming in Nigeria represents a lucrative business opportunity that aligns with current trends in health-conscious consumer choices and sustainable agricultural practices.

16. SOYBEAN FARMING AND TRADING

This presents lucrative opportunities for entrepreneurs in Nigeria, given the versatile uses of soybeans in various industries. Here's a discussion on both aspects:

- *Soybean Farming:*

Soybean farming is a profitable venture due to the high demand for soybean products globally. Soybeans are rich in protein and oil, making them essential in animal feed, food processing, and the production of soy-based products. Nigeria's climate is favourable for soybean cultivation, and the crop is known for its nitrogen-fixing properties, which benefit soil fertility. Entrepreneurs in soybean farming can tap into both domestic and international markets, contributing to food security and economic growth. Additionally, soybean farming can be integrated into sustainable agricultural practices, promoting crop rotation and reducing dependence on synthetic fertilizers.

- *Soybean Trading:*

Soybean trading involves buying soybeans from farmers and selling them to processors or end-users. Entrepreneurs can operate as middlemen, connecting farmers with buyers, or establish a soybean trading business that involves purchasing, processing, and selling soybean products. The demand for soybean products in Nigeria and beyond creates ample opportunities for traders to participate in the supply chain. Market demand, pricing trends, and supply chain efficiency all have an impact on soybean trading profits. Developing strategic partnerships with farmers, processors, and distributors can enhance the success of a soybean trading business.

Challenges and Considerations:

While soybean farming and trading offer significant opportunities, entrepreneurs should be aware of challenges such as price fluctuations, market volatility, and the need for proper storage facilities to prevent post-harvest losses. Adequate knowledge of soybean cultivation practices, market dynamics, and trade regulations is crucial for success in this business. Moreover, staying informed about global trends in soybean production and consumption can provide a competitive edge in the trading aspect of the business.

In summary, both soybean farming and trading in Nigeria present promising prospects for entrepreneurs. The key lies in adopting efficient farming practices, understanding market dynamics, and establishing robust connections within the soybean supply chain to ensure a successful and sustainable business venture.

17. GINGER AND GARLIC FARMING

Ginger and garlic farming in Nigeria can be a lucrative business due to the high demand for these spices in local and international markets. To start, assess soil conditions and ensure well-drained and fertile land. Implementing organic farming practices can enhance the quality of the produce.

Consider climate factors, as ginger and garlic thrive in tropical climates. Adequate irrigation and mulching can help maintain soil moisture. Utilise quality seeds and proper spacing for optimal yield. Regular monitoring for pests and diseases is essential; organic pest control methods are preferred to maintain product quality.

Market research is crucial to understanding demand trends. Establishing relationships with local markets, supermarkets, and exporters can ensure a steady income. Additionally, value-added products like powdered ginger and garlic can diversify revenue streams.

Overall, ginger and garlic farming can be a rewarding venture in Nigeria with careful planning, sustainable practices, and market awareness.

18. RETAIL BUSINESS (e.g., grocery store, boutique)

Starting a retail business in Nigeria, whether a grocery store or boutique, requires a comprehensive understanding of the local market dynamics. Entrepreneurs should conduct thorough market research to identify consumer preferences, purchasing behaviours, and competition. Establishing a reliable supply chain for products is crucial to ensuring a consistent inventory and competitive pricing.

Navigating regulatory requirements and obtaining necessary permits are essential steps for a smooth business operation. Additionally, embracing technology for inventory management and customer engagement can enhance the efficiency and competitiveness of the retail business. Creating a welcoming and culturally sensitive shopping environment, along with providing excellent customer service, can foster customer loyalty in the diverse and dynamic Nigerian market. Overall, a well-planned approach, adaptability to local conditions, and a customer-centric focus can contribute to the success of a retail business in Nigeria.

19. COSMETICS AND BEAUTY SUPPLY STORE

Starting a cosmetics and beauty supply store in Nigeria presents a promising business opportunity, given the country's growing beauty industry. Conducting market research is crucial to understanding consumer preferences, popular brands, and emerging trends. Focus on offering a diverse range of products to cater to a broad customer base, considering both local and international brands.

Location plays a significant role in the success of a cosmetics store. Choosing a strategic and accessible location can attract more foot traffic. Establishing relationships with distributors and suppliers to ensure a consistent and quality product supply is key. Additionally, creating an engaging online presence can broaden the customer reach and facilitate e-commerce transactions.

Providing personalised customer service, hosting beauty events, and offering loyalty programmes can enhance customer retention. Staying updated on beauty trends and incorporating them into the product selection can keep the store competitive. Adhering to regulatory requirements and maintaining high hygiene standards are also essential considerations for a successful cosmetics and beauty supply store in Nigeria.

20. MOBILE PHONE ACCESSORIES SHOP

Running a mobile phone accessories shop can be lucrative in Nigeria for several reasons. Firstly, Nigeria has a large and growing mobile phone market, with an increasing number of people owning smartphones. This creates a consistent demand for accessories such as chargers, cases, headphones, and screen protectors.

Additionally, Nigeria's tech-savvy youth are keen on staying updated with the latest gadgets and accessories. The rapid pace of technological advancements and the desire for personalisation contribute to a continuous demand for innovative and trendy accessories.

Furthermore, the mobile phone accessories business allows for diverse product offerings at various price points, catering to different consumer segments. Establishing an online presence and leveraging social media can expand the customer base beyond the physical store. Overall, the combination of a booming mobile phone market, tech-savvy demographics, and a diverse product range makes a mobile phone accessories shop a potentially lucrative venture in Nigeria.

21. MOBILE GAS VENDING

Mobile gas vending can be a lucrative business in Nigeria due to the increasing demand for cooking gas. By providing convenient and efficient delivery services to homes and businesses, you can capitalise on the following factors:

1. *Convenience:* Offering doorstep delivery of cooking gas saves customers time and effort, making your service more appealing than traditional methods.
2. *Market Demand*: With Nigeria's rising population and urbanisation, the demand for clean cooking fuel like LPG (liquefied petroleum gas) is growing, creating a substantial market for mobile gas vendors.

3. *Safety and Compliance:* Emphasise strict adherence to safety standards and regulations, gaining trust among customers. Ensuring compliance with safety measures will attract more clients who prioritise secure gas handling.

4. *Technology Integration:* Use technology for order tracking, online payments, and efficient route planning. This will streamline operations and enhance the customer experience.

5. *Marketing Strategies*: Implement targeted marketing campaigns to create awareness about your mobile gas vending service. Highlight the convenience, safety, and reliability of your business to attract a wider customer base.

6. *Partnerships:* Collaborate with local businesses, real estate developers, and event organisers to expand your reach. Establishing partnerships can lead to bulk orders and increased visibility.

7. *Government Support:* Stay current on government initiatives and policies that promote clean energy. Leveraging these incentives can give you a competitive edge and contribute to the growth of your business.

8. *Customer Education:* Offer resources and materials to educate customers about the benefits of using LPG, dispelling any myths or misconceptions. Informed customers are more likely to choose your service.

9. *Environmental Impact:* Emphasise the eco-friendly nature of LPG as a clean cooking fuel. Appeal to environmentally conscious consumers who are looking for sustainable alternatives.

By focusing on these aspects and providing excellent customer service, a mobile gas vending business has the potential to thrive in Nigeria's evolving market. This business model is simple: Many people find it stressful and time-consuming to carry gas cylinders around whenever they want to refill, especially people who do not have personal vehicles, so you simply bring gas to their doorsteps and get paid a little extra for the home service.

Hypothetically, I want to consider two classes of people in this kind of business according to financial strength.

A. **A lower-class businessman:** This is someone with less than 3 million Naira who wants to engage in this kind of business. He can get a bike and a single 50kg gas cylinder, go to a mega gas station, fill it and deliver from door to door. Most people would prefer a gas vendor to drive to their doorstep, where they can simply bring out their gas cylinders and have them refilled. They would not mind paying extra as far as it will ease off the stress of travelling to a gas station and waiting till it gets to their turn to refill. Such a vendor could simply print stickers with his contact details so that customers could call him whenever they need a refill. If he adds only 100 Naira per kg to the price with which he bought at the mega station, he makes 5,000 Naira per 50kg cylinder. The quantity he sells daily will depend on the number of customers he has or is able to gather.

B. **A middle-class businessman/businesswoman:** I deliberately designed this one to include women because its nature would not require that the owner directly go around carrying gas cylinders on a bike. The persons that fall under this category are people who can afford a mini gas station with all the necessary machines and are able to buy two or more cargo tricycles for supplies; he/she must have above 10 million Naira to be able to engage in this kind of activity. This one requires that people are employed to go out with the tricycles, and each crew can carry three or more 50kg gas cylinders. This enables them to go to even remote areas of town to supply gas to individual homes. This kind enables the person to acquire a large market share and make more volumes of sales per time.

22. ESTABLISHING AN ELECTRONICS REPAIR SHOP

Establishing an Electronics Repair Shop can be a lucrative venture for several reasons.

1. *Growing Electronics Market:* With technology continuously evolving, the demand for electronic devices remains high. As more people own smartphones, laptops, tablets, and other gadgets, the need for repair services increases, providing a consistent customer base.
2. *Cost-Effective Repairs:* Many consumers prefer repairing their devices rather than replacing them due to cost considerations. Offering affordable repair services can attract customers looking for budget-friendly solutions, making your shop a go-to option.
3. *Specialised Expertise:* As an Electronics Repair Shop owner, having skilled technicians with expertise in repairing various devices is crucial. Providing specialised services for a range of electronics sets your business apart, attracting customers who need specific and knowledgeable assistance.
4. *Environmental Consciousness*: Repairing electronics aligns with the growing trend of environmental consciousness. People are increasingly seeking ways to reduce electronic waste, and repairing devices instead of discarding them contributes to sustainability, making your business more appealing.
5. *Quick Turnaround Time:* Providing efficient and timely repair services can lead to customer satisfaction and repeat business. Establishing a system that prioritises quick

turnaround times ensures positive reviews and word-of-mouth referrals.

6. *Diversification of Services:* Expanding your services beyond common repairs, such as offering software troubleshooting, upgrades, and data recovery, can broaden your customer base. Providing a one-stop shop for various electronic needs enhances your business's attractiveness.
7. *Local Community Presence:* Building a strong presence in your local community through effective marketing and community engagement can establish trust and credibility. People often prefer local businesses for their convenience and personalised service.
8. *Warranty and Guarantees:* Offering warranties and guarantees on repairs instils confidence in customers and demonstrates your commitment to quality service. This can lead to increased customer loyalty and positive reviews, which are crucial in a service-oriented industry.
9. *Adaptability to Market Trends:* Staying updated on the latest technological trends and adapting your services accordingly ensures that your business remains relevant. Being able to repair the latest gadgets and address emerging issues can attract tech-savvy customers.
10. *Partnerships with Retailers:* Establishing partnerships with local retailers or electronic stores for referrals can help in attracting a steady stream of customers. Collaboration can create a win-win situation, benefiting both parties.

In conclusion, an Electronics Repair Shop can be profitable by catering for the growing demand for electronics repair services, providing cost-effective solutions, specialising in expertise, and adapting to market trends. Building a trustworthy and customer-oriented business is key to long-term success in this industry.

23. FASHION DESIGN AND TAILORING BUSINESS

The fashion industry is dynamic and ever-evolving, offering countless opportunities for entrepreneurs to thrive. A particularly promising avenue within this sector is the Fashion Design and Tailoring business. This book explores the intricacies of this industry and delves into the reasons why it has the potential to catapult individuals into millionaire status within a few years.

1. *Growing Market and Consumer Demand:* The global fashion industry is continuously expanding, fueled by changing consumer preferences and a desire for unique, personalised clothing. Establishing a Fashion Design and Tailoring business taps into this growing market, catering to individuals who seek custom-made garments that reflect their style and personality.
2. *Unique and Personalised Offerings:* Unlike mass-produced clothing, a fashion design and tailoring business allows entrepreneurs to offer bespoke and personalised creations. This uniqueness not only attracts customers but also justifies premium pricing, contributing to higher profit margins.
3. *E-commerce and Global Reach:* The advent of e-commerce has transformed the fashion landscape, providing opportunities for businesses to reach a global audience. Establishing an online presence enables entrepreneurs to showcase their designs and attract customers worldwide, significantly increasing the potential for substantial profits.
4. *Celebrity and Influencer Collaborations:* Collaborating with celebrities or influencers can propel a fashion design and tailoring business into the spotlight. Social media platforms provide a powerful marketing tool, allowing entrepreneurs

to showcase their designs to a vast audience and drive brand recognition and sales.

5. *Innovation and Trendsetting:* Staying ahead of fashion trends and introducing innovative designs sets a business apart in a competitive market. Entrepreneurs who demonstrate a keen sense of style and an ability to set trends are more likely to attract a dedicated customer base, leading to increased revenue.
6. *Luxury and High-End Markets:* Targeting the luxury and high-end markets can be a lucrative strategy. Affluent consumers are willing to pay a premium for exclusive, high-quality garments, and establishing a reputation for luxury and craftsmanship can result in significant financial gains.
7. *Diversification of Services:* Beyond traditional tailoring, diversifying services to include bridal wear, formal attire, or thematic collections can expand the customer base. Specialising in specific niches allows entrepreneurs to cater to different markets and capitalise on diverse revenue streams.
8. *Quality Craftsmanship and Materials:* Emphasising quality craftsmanship and the use of premium materials adds value to the products. Customers are often willing to pay more for well-made, durable garments, contributing to a positive reputation and repeat business.
9. *Networking and Industry Connections:* Building strong connections within the fashion industry can open doors to collaborations, partnerships, and opportunities for growth. Networking with suppliers, other designers, and industry influencers can provide valuable insights and support for business expansion.

10. *Adaptability to Sustainable Practices:* With increasing awareness of environmental issues, adopting sustainable and ethical practices in the fashion business is not only socially responsible but also appeals to eco-conscious consumers. Entrepreneurs who integrate sustainability into their business models can attract a broader customer base and enhance profitability.

The Fashion Design and Tailoring business holds immense potential for aspiring entrepreneurs to achieve millionaire status in a relatively short timeframe. By tapping into the growing market, offering personalised and unique creations, embracing e-commerce, and staying ahead of trends, individuals can build a successful and lucrative business. With dedication, creativity, and a strategic approach, the path to millionaire success in the fashion industry becomes a realistic and achievable goal.

24. FOOTWEAR MANUFACTURING

Footwear manufacturing stands out as a lucrative business option in the modern-day economy due to its inherent resilience and adaptability. In a world marked by economic uncertainties, the consistent demand for shoes across diverse consumer segments provides a stable market foundation. The industry's ability to diversify into athletic, casual, formal, and specialised footwear caters to varied consumer preferences, ensuring relevance in ever-evolving fashion trends.

Furthermore, the global nature of the footwear market offers opportunities for expansion and reduces dependence on specific economic conditions in one region. The rise of e-commerce aligns seamlessly with footwear manufacturing, allowing direct access to consumers and efficient distribution channels.

Focusing on branding, innovation, and sustainable practices puts footwear manufacturers at the forefront of consumer awareness. By staying attuned to fashion trends and incorporating customisable options, the industry maintains consumer interest and loyalty. Moreover, the adaptability of footwear manufacturers to supply chain optimisation contributes to cost-effectiveness, a crucial factor in navigating economic fluctuations.

In summary, the Footwear Manufacturing business thrives in the modern economy by capitalising on steady demand, diversification, global reach, e-commerce trends, branding, innovation, and sustainability. Its resilience and ability to align with contemporary consumer expectations make it a compelling and enduring option for entrepreneurs seeking a stable and profitable venture.

25. JEWELLERY MAKING AND SALES

Jewellery making and sales present a compelling opportunity for Nigerians, particularly women, to establish a lucrative source of income. The cultural significance of jewellery in Nigeria, combined with changing consumer preferences and economic dynamics, creates a favourable environment for success in this industry.

Firstly, Nigeria boasts of a rich cultural heritage that places significant value on adornment and jewellery. Traditional ceremonies, festivals, and everyday wear often involve the use of jewellery, showcasing a robust market with consistent demand. Women, in particular, can leverage their creativity and craftsmanship in jewellery-making to meet this demand. The ability to create unique, culturally inspired pieces allows for a personalised touch that resonates with customers. This not only caters to local tastes but also positions the business for potential international appeal, contributing to global market access.

The rise of e-commerce and digital marketing provides an avenue for women in the jewellery business to showcase and sell their creations beyond local markets. Online platforms enable entrepreneurs to reach a broader audience, tapping into the growing trend of online shopping.

Moreover, the relatively low entry barriers in jewellery-making make it an accessible business option. Women can start small, gradually expanding their operations as they gain experience and build a customer base. This scalability aligns with the economic realities faced by many aspiring entrepreneurs.

In terms of economic empowerment, a successful jewellery business can significantly contribute to household income, financial independence, and community development. By providing employment opportunities, particularly for other women, entrepreneurs contribute to local economic growth.

The timeless nature of these accessories further enhances the sustainability of the jewellery industry. Jewellery tends to retain or appreciate in value over time, making it a wise investment for both creators and buyers. This longevity adds a layer of financial security to the venture.

26. BOOKSTORE OR STATIONERY SHOP

Establishing a bookstore or stationery shop in Nigeria can be a viable and rewarding business that caters to the educational and office needs of the population. When considering suitable locations for such a venture, several factors come into play:

1. *Proximity to Educational Institutions:* It is strategic to locate the bookstore or stationery shop in close proximity to schools, colleges, and universities. These areas create a steady demand for textbooks, notebooks, and various stationery

items, making it a convenient option for students and faculty.

2. *Commercial Districts and Business Centres:* Placing the store in commercial districts or areas with a concentration of businesses is advantageous. Such locations attract professionals and office workers who frequently require stationery supplies, creating a consistent customer base.

3. *Residential Areas with High Population Density:* Densely populated residential areas should be considered. Families and individuals in these communities often require stationery items for home offices, school-going children, or personal use.

4. *Proximity to Government Institutions:* Locating the store near government offices or institutions can be beneficial. Government offices typically have administrative and educational requirements, driving demand for stationery and office supplies.

5. *Shopping Malls and Commercial Complexes:* Setting up within shopping malls or commercial complexes provides exposure to a diverse customer base. The foot traffic in these areas can lead to increased visibility and sales, especially if the store offers a variety of products beyond books and stationery.

6. *Transportation Hubs:* Areas around transportation hubs, such as bus terminals, train stations, or airports, can attract a transient customer base. Travellers often require reading materials and stationery items, presenting an additional market segment.

7. *Tech and Business Parks:* Consideration should be given to areas with technology parks or business hubs. Professionals working in these environments may require specialised

stationery, notebooks, or business-related books, presenting an opportunity for niche offerings.

8. *Tourist Areas:* In tourist destinations, offering a selection of books, travel guides, and souvenirs can attract both local and international customers. Including stationery items can cater to the needs of travellers and those looking for unique gifts.
9. *Proximity to Libraries and Educational Centres:* Locating the store near libraries or educational centres complements these institutions. Students and researchers visiting libraries may need additional materials, creating a convenient option nearby.
10. *Online Presence and Delivery Services:* While physical location is crucial, considering an online presence with delivery services can broaden the business's reach. This allows customers to order books and stationery items from the comfort of their homes, expanding the potential customer base.

In summary, a Bookstore or Stationery Shop in Nigeria can thrive by strategically locating the business in areas with high educational and commercial activity. Proximity to schools, businesses, government institutions, and transportation hubs, along with a thoughtful online presence, contribute to the venture's success.

27. HOME DECOR AND FURNISHING

Home decor and furnishing are lucrative business ventures in Nigeria, fueled by a burgeoning middle class, increasing urbanisation, and a growing desire for aesthetically pleasing living spaces. The demand for stylish and functional home goods has led to the emergence of successful companies in this sector, showcasing the industry's profitability.

One key factor contributing to the profitability of the Home Decor and Furnishing business in Nigeria is the cultural emphasis on home aesthetics and hospitality. Nigerians take pride in creating welcoming and visually appealing homes, driving a consistent demand for furniture, decor items, and interior design services.

Major players in the Nigerian home decor market, such as Vitafoam Nigeria Plc and Mouka Limited, have capitalised on this demand by offering a diverse range of quality furniture and bedding products. These companies have not only established themselves as household names but also demonstrated the potential for long-term success in the industry.

The real estate boom in urban centres like Lagos and Abuja further fuels the demand for home decor and furnishing. As individuals invest in new homes or renovate existing ones, the need for contemporary and functional furniture, lighting, and decor becomes paramount, providing ample opportunities for businesses in this sector.

Moreover, the rise of interior design as a sought-after service has opened new avenues for entrepreneurs. Companies like Homely NG have successfully combined e-commerce platforms with interior design expertise, offering customers a seamless experience in transforming their living spaces. The increasing influence of global design trends, facilitated by digital connectivity, has also played a role in shaping consumer preferences. Businesses that stay abreast of international design trends and offer products aligned with these preferences can capture a broader market share.

The shift towards online retail further underscores the potential for growth in the Home Decor and Furnishing business.

Companies like Jumia and Konga have successfully entered the e-commerce space, providing customers with a wide array of home decor and furnishing products through their online platforms.

Home Decor and Furnishing represent a profitable business venture in Nigeria due to the cultural importance placed on home aesthetics, the real estate boom, the influence of global design trends, and the increasing popularity of online retail. Successful companies in this sector have demonstrated the market's potential for sustained growth, making it an attractive opportunity for entrepreneurs looking to tap into Nigeria's evolving consumer landscape.

28. AUTO PARTS SALES

This is one business I love so much and will always do. I currently operate as an authorised dealer of TVS tricycle spare parts, and the experience has been great and delightful. The Igbo tribe of Nigeria dominates this particular aspect of business, and these people are not only majors in this business in Nigeria but also in most African countries.

1. *Current Landscape:* The auto parts sales business in Nigeria is a thriving industry fueled by the country's growing automotive market and the need for replacement parts. The dominance of this sector is largely attributed to a mix of local entrepreneurs, importers, and established businesses that have capitalised on the demand for quality auto parts.
2. *Key Players:* Several dominant players characterise the landscape of the auto parts sales industry in Nigeria. Local entrepreneurs and family-owned businesses often play a significant role, establishing themselves as reliable suppliers within their communities. Importers, leveraging

international connections, contribute to the availability of a diverse range of auto parts.

3. *Challenges and Opportunities:* Despite the industry's growth, challenges persist. Counterfeit parts, a common concern, undermine the integrity of the market and pose risks to consumers. Additionally, a notable gap exists in the accessibility of genuine, high-quality auto parts, especially in remote areas. This gap presents an opportunity for new entrants to address the demand for reliable and authentic components.

4. *Need for More Players:* The auto parts sales business in Nigeria stands to benefit from the entry of more entrepreneurs and businesses. Here's why:

28.1. Diversification of Offerings

The introduction of new players can lead to a more diverse range of products and services. Specialised businesses can emerge, focusing on specific types of auto parts or catering to niche markets, addressing the varying needs of consumers.

28.2. Enhanced Competition and Pricing:

Increased competition often results in competitive pricing and improved services. New entrants can bring fresh perspectives and innovative strategies, fostering a healthier business environment that benefits both sellers and consumers.

28.3. Geographical Expansion:

Many parts of Nigeria, particularly in rural or less urbanised areas, still face challenges in accessing quality auto parts. The entry of new businesses can contribute to the geographical expansion of the industry, ensuring that a broader population has access to essential components.

28.4. Technology Integration:

The auto parts sales business can benefit from technology integration, such as online platforms, e-commerce, and efficient inventory management systems. New entrants with a focus on leveraging technology can enhance the industry's overall efficiency and customer experience.

28.5. Quality Assurance and Consumer Trust:

Trust in the authenticity and quality of auto parts is crucial. New entrants who prioritise genuine products and transparent business practices can contribute to building consumer trust, helping to mitigate concerns related to counterfeit parts.

28.6. Job Creation and Economic Impact:

The expansion of the auto parts sales industry through new entrants creates jobs and has an economic impact. More businesses mean more employment opportunities, fostering local economic development.

In conclusion, while existing players, especially the Igbos, dominate the auto parts sales business in Nigeria, there is a clear need for more entrepreneurs and businesses to enter the market. This industry presents opportunities for diversification, enhanced competition, geographical expansion, technology integration, and improved consumer trust. New entrants have the potential to contribute significantly to the growth and sustainability of the auto parts sales business in Nigeria.

29. RESTAURANT OR FAST FOOD BUSINESS

The prospects for the restaurant and fast food business in Nigeria are promising, driven by factors such as a growing urban population, changing lifestyles, and an increasing preference for dining out. The country's diverse culinary culture and rising middle class contribute to a thriving food service industry.

Current Business Leaders:

Several notable players dominate the restaurant and fast food sector in Nigeria:

1. Chicken Republic

A leading fast-food chain, Chicken Republic is renowned for its fried chicken and diverse menu offerings. With a strong presence across Nigeria, it exemplifies the success achievable in the fast-food business.

2. Tantalizers

Tantalizers is a well-established brand in the Nigerian fast food industry. It offers a range of local and international dishes. The company's widespread presence reflects its adaptability to local tastes.

3. KFC

The global giant KFC has successfully expanded its footprint in Nigeria. Known for its popular chicken products, KFC demonstrates the appeal of internationally recognised brands in the Nigerian market.

Entering and Growing in Business:

For small business owners looking to enter and grow in the restaurant or fast food business in Nigeria, several strategies can contribute to success:

1. Market Research and Niche Identification: Conduct thorough market research to identify gaps or underserved

niches. Specialising in a particular cuisine or offering unique menu items can set a small business apart from competitors.

2. Location Selection: Choose a strategic location based on target demographics and foot traffic. High-visibility areas, commercial districts, or proximity to residential neighbourhoods can enhance the restaurant's visibility and accessibility.

3. Quality and Consistency: Prioritise the quality and consistency of food offerings. Establishing a reputation for delicious and reliable cuisine encourages repeat business and positive word-of-mouth, which is crucial for growth.

4. Incorporate Local Flavours: Embrace local flavours and ingredients to cater to the diverse tastes of the Nigerian population. A blend of international and local dishes can appeal to a broader customer base.

5. Invest in Marketing and Branding: Utilise effective marketing strategies, both online and offline, to create awareness. Building a strong brand identity, including a visually appealing logo and consistent branding across platforms, contributes to customer recognition.

6. Technology Integration: Embrace technology for online ordering, delivery services, and efficient management systems. A user-friendly website or mobile app can enhance the customer experience and attract a tech-savvy audience.

7. Customer Engagement: Prioritise customer engagement through social media, loyalty programmes, and feedback mechanisms. Building a connection with customers fosters loyalty and can lead to positive reviews and recommendations.

8. Cost Management: Implement effective cost management practices to ensure profitability. Efficient inventory

management, waste reduction, and negotiating favourable deals with suppliers all contribute to financial sustainability.

9. Training and Staff Development: Invest in training for staff to maintain high standards of service. A well-trained and motivated team contributes to a positive dining experience, encouraging customer loyalty.

10. Adaptability and Innovation: Stay adaptable to changing market trends and continuously innovate. Introducing new menu items, promotions, or seasonal offerings keeps the business dynamic and appealing to customers.

The restaurant and fast food business in Nigeria holds considerable prospects for small business owners. By conducting thorough research, focusing on quality, embracing local flavours, and implementing effective marketing and technology strategies, entrepreneurs can enter and comfortably grow in this dynamic and flourishing industry.

30. BAKERY

The bakery business in Nigeria is a potential goldmine, driven by a number of factors that make it a profitable venture in the country's dynamic market.

1. *Growing Population and Urbanisation:* Nigeria's population is rapidly growing, and urbanisation is on the rise. As more people move to urban areas, the demand for convenient and ready-to-eat food items, including bakery products, experiences a considerable surge.

2. *Cultural Significance of Baked Goods:* Baked goods, such as bread, pastries, and snacks, hold significant cultural importance in Nigeria. Bread is a staple in the Nigerian diet, making the bakery business a fundamental part of daily life.

This cultural affinity ensures a consistent and widespread demand for bakery products.

3. *Breakfast and Snacking Culture:* Nigeria's breakfast and snacking culture further accentuates the viability of a bakery business. With a preference for quick, on-the-go options, bakeries that offer a variety of fresh and tasty products cater to the needs of a fast-paced population.
4. *Job Creation and Economic Impact:* Establishing a bakery not only taps into the economic potential of the food industry but also contributes to job creation. Bakeries, whether small-scale or large, provide employment opportunities, fostering economic development at the local level.
5. *Diverse Product Offerings:* The versatility of bakery products allows for diverse offerings. Beyond traditional bread, bakeries can explore a range of products, including cakes, pastries, cookies, and speciality items. This diversity caters to different consumer preferences, expanding the customer base.
6. *Specialised and Niche Markets:* Bakeries can tap into specialised and niche markets by offering gluten-free, organic, or artisanal baked goods. Addressing specific dietary preferences or health-conscious consumer demands presents an opportunity for differentiation and premium pricing.
7. *Events and Celebrations Market:* Numerous celebrations and events mark Nigeria's vibrant culture. Bakeries can capitalise on this by offering customised cakes and pastries for birthdays, weddings, and other special occasions, creating a lucrative niche market.
8. *Rise of Online Ordering and Delivery:* The increasing use of online platforms for food ordering and delivery has become

a significant trend in Nigeria. Bakeries can leverage this by establishing an online presence, partnering with delivery services, and reaching a broader customer base beyond physical store locations.

9. *Branding and Marketing Opportunities:* Effective branding and marketing strategies can elevate a bakery's visibility. Creative packaging, engaging social media campaigns, and collaborations with influencers can enhance brand recognition and attract a loyal customer base.

10. *Adaptability to Health Trends:* With a growing awareness of health and wellness, bakeries can adapt by incorporating healthier ingredients, offering whole-grain options, or introducing low-sugar and gluten-free products. Aligning with health trends can attract health-conscious consumers.

In conclusion, the bakery business in Nigeria represents a potential goldmine due to the country's demographic trends, the cultural significance of baked goods, diverse product offerings, and the industry's adaptability to changing consumer preferences. Entrepreneurs entering the bakery business can tap into this goldmine by combining traditional favourites with innovative approaches, meeting the evolving demands of Nigeria's dynamic market.

31. CATERING SERVICES

Catering services in Nigeria have seen significant growth due to the country's diverse cultural events and social gatherings. The demand for professional catering has risen, with businesses offering a range of services, from weddings to corporate events. Factors such as food quality, presentation, and customer service play crucial roles in the success of catering ventures. Additionally, adapting to cultural preferences and ensuring compliance with health and safety regulations are essential for sustained success in the Nigerian catering industry.

32. ICE CREAM SHOP

An ice cream shop in Nigeria can achieve financial success by focusing on several key strategies. Firstly, offering a diverse range of flavours, including locally inspired options, can attract a wider customer base. Strategic location, particularly in areas with high foot traffic or near popular recreational spots, can enhance visibility. Engaging in effective marketing through social media and partnerships with local businesses can also boost brand awareness. Additionally, maintaining consistent quality, providing a pleasant ambience, and incorporating innovative offerings or promotions can contribute to customer loyalty and increased revenue for the ice cream shop.

33. OPERATING A SMOOTHIE AND JUICE BAR:

This business involves several key elements for success.

1. *Market Research:* Conduct thorough market research to identify target demographics, preferences, and competitors in the chosen location. Understand the demand for health-conscious beverages.
2. *Menu Development:* Create a diverse menu offering a variety of smoothies and juices, incorporating both classic and unique flavours. Consider catering to dietary preferences and offering customisable options.
3. *Quality Ingredients:* Source fresh, high-quality fruits and vegetables. Emphasise organic and locally sourced ingredients to appeal to health-conscious consumers.

4. *Equipment and Layout:* Invest in quality blenders and juicers. Design an inviting and efficient bar layout to enhance customer experience. Consider seating arrangements for customers who prefer to enjoy their drinks on-site.

5. *Branding and Marketing:* Develop a strong brand identity with an appealing logo and branding materials. Utilise social media platforms to showcase products, share health benefits and engage with the community. Offer promotions and loyalty programmes to attract and retain customers.

6. *Health and Safety Compliance:* Adhere to health and safety regulations, ensuring cleanliness and proper food handling practices. Display nutritional information to cater to health-conscious consumers.

7. *Customer Engagement:* Foster a welcoming atmosphere and provide excellent customer service. Encourage customer feedback and use it to improve offerings. Consider hosting events or workshops related to health and wellness.

8. *Partnerships:* To expand reach, explore partnerships with gyms, wellness centres, or local businesses. Collaborate with influencers or fitness enthusiasts to promote the brand.

9. *Innovation:* Stay updated on health trends and continuously innovate the menu with new, nutritious options. Introduce seasonal specials to keep offerings fresh and exciting.

10. *Sustainability:* Consider eco-friendly practices, such as using biodegradable cups and straws, to align with sustainability trends.

11. *Financial Management:* Maintain a solid financial plan, including budgeting for ingredients, marketing, and operational costs. Monitor sales trends and adjust the menu or promotions accordingly.

A successful Smoothie and Juice Bar business requires a combination of a well-designed menu, effective marketing, commitment to quality, and a focus on customer satisfaction to thrive in the competitive beverage industry.

34. SNACK VENDING

Starting a Snack Vending business in Nigeria involves several considerations for success.

1. *Market Research:* Conduct thorough market research to identify high-traffic locations, target demographics, and popular snack preferences in different regions of Nigeria.
2. *Product Selection:* Offer a diverse range of snacks that cater to local tastes while also including international options—create a balance between healthy and indulgent choices to appeal to a broad audience.
3. *Location Strategy:* Choose strategic locations with high foot traffic, such as offices, schools, and busy commercial areas. Negotiate partnerships with businesses to place vending machines on their premises.
4. *Quality and Freshness:* Ensure that snacks are fresh, well-packaged, and meet quality standards. Regularly restock machines to maintain a positive customer experience.
5. *Technology Integration:* Consider incorporating modern vending machine technology, such as cashless payment options and inventory tracking systems, to enhance efficiency and convenience.
6. *Regulatory Compliance:* Adhere to health and safety regulations, obtaining necessary permits and certifications for operating vending machines.

7. *Marketing and Branding:* Implement eye-catching branding on vending machines to attract attention: Utilise digital platforms and social media to promote the vending business and any special promotions.
8. *Customer Engagement:* Implement customer feedback mechanisms to understand preferences and improve offerings. Consider loyalty programmes or discounts for repeat customers.
9. *Maintenance and Service:* Establish a regular maintenance schedule to ensure vending machines are in optimal working condition. Respond quickly to any malfunctions or customer concerns.
10. *Cost Management:* Develop a sound financial plan, including pricing strategies that balance profitability with affordability for customers.
11. *Monitoring and Analytics:* Utilise analytics tools to track sales trends, popular products, and machine performance. Use this data to optimise product selection and placement.
12. *Security Measures:* Implement security features on vending machines to prevent theft or vandalism. Choose well-lit and secure locations to minimise risks.

A Snack Vending business in Nigeria can be lucrative when carefully planned and executed, considering local preferences, optimal locations, and a focus on quality and customer satisfaction. Regularly adapting to market trends and leveraging technology can contribute to long-term success in the snack vending industry.

35. LOCAL CUISINE RESTAURANT

A local cuisine restaurant business in Nigeria involves showcasing and serving traditional Nigerian dishes, reflecting the rich and diverse culinary heritage of the country. Here are key aspects to consider:

- *Culinary Offering:*

Provide a menu featuring a variety of local dishes from different regions of Nigeria. Include popular staples like jollof rice, pounded yam with egusi soup, suya, moi moi, and other regional specialities. Offer vegetarian and non-vegetarian options to cater to diverse preferences.

- *Authenticity and Quality:*

Maintain authenticity in recipe preparation and use high-quality, locally sourced ingredients. Emphasise traditional cooking methods and flavours to ensure an authentic dining experience for customers.

- *Ambiance and Decor:*

Create an inviting atmosphere that reflects Nigerian culture through decor, artwork, and music. Consider incorporating traditional elements to enhance the overall dining experience.

- *Cultural Events and Festivals:*

Organise events or theme nights celebrating Nigerian festivals, cultural events, or holidays. This can attract a broader audience and create a sense of community around the restaurant.

- *Local Partnerships:*

Establish relationships with local farmers and suppliers to ensure a fresh and consistent supply of ingredients. Collaborate with local businesses and artisans for unique offerings or decor.

- *Customer Engagement:*

Encourage customer feedback to understand preferences and continually improve the menu. Consider offering cooking classes or demonstrations to engage with the community and share the culinary culture.

- *Marketing and Promotion:*

Utilise social media platforms to showcase the restaurant's atmosphere, dishes, and special events. Leverage online reviews and testimonials to build credibility and attract a wider customer base.

- *Health and Safety Compliance:*

Adhere to health and safety regulations to maintain a clean and safe dining environment. Display nutritional information and allergen details for transparency.

- *Staff Training:*

Train staff to provide excellent customer service and educate them about the significance of each dish. Friendly and knowledgeable staff contribute to a positive dining experience.

- *Adaptability:*

Stay adaptable to changing food trends and customer preferences. Introduce seasonal variations or modern twists to traditional dishes to keep the menu fresh and appealing.

- *Community Involvement:*

Engage with the local community by sponsoring events, participating in local festivals, or supporting charitable causes. This can enhance the restaurant's reputation and foster community loyalty.

Successfully running a Local Cuisine Restaurant in Nigeria involves a blend of culinary expertise, cultural sensitivity, and effective business strategies. By offering an authentic experience, building community connections, and maintaining high standards, such a restaurant can thrive in the diverse and vibrant culinary landscape of Nigeria.

36. FOOD DELIVERY SERVICES BUSINESS

A Food Delivery Services business in Nigeria involves facilitating the delivery of food from restaurants to customers' locations. Here's a brief overview:

- *Ordering Platform:*

Establish an online platform or mobile app where customers can browse restaurant menus, place orders, and make payments seamlessly. Ensure a user-friendly interface to enhance the overall customer experience.

- *Restaurant Partnerships:*

Collaborate with a variety of local restaurants to expand the range of cuisines available for delivery. Build strong partnerships to ensure timely order processing and maintain a diverse menu.

- *Delivery Logistics:*

Develop an efficient delivery system with a fleet of delivery personnel or through partnerships with third-party delivery services. Focus on timely and secure deliveries to enhance customer satisfaction.

- *Technology Integration:*

Leverage technology for order tracking, real-time updates, and communication with customers. Implement features such as GPS tracking to provide transparency throughout the delivery process.

- *Marketing and Promotions:*

Advertise the food delivery service through online and offline channels. Offer promotions, discounts, or loyalty programmes to attract and retain customers. Collaborate with restaurants for joint marketing efforts.

- *Customer Support:*

Provide responsive customer support to address queries, concerns, or issues promptly. A reliable customer support system enhances user trust and loyalty.

- *Payment Options:*

Offer a variety of secure and convenient payment options to cater to diverse customer preferences. Ensure transparent pricing and communicate any additional fees clearly.

- *Quality Control:*

Establish standards for food quality during transit to maintain the integrity of dishes. Implement temperature-controlled packaging and guidelines for restaurants to follow when preparing orders for delivery.

- *Health and Safety Compliance:*

Adhere to health and safety regulations for food handling and delivery. Conduct regular inspections of restaurant partners to ensure compliance with hygiene standards.

- *Geographic Coverage:*

Expand the service's geographic coverage gradually to reach a wider audience. Prioritise areas with high population density and demand for food delivery.

- *Data Analytics:*

Utilise data analytics to understand customer preferences, optimise delivery routes, and make informed business decisions. Insights from data can also help tailor promotions and improve service efficiency.

A Food Delivery Services business in Nigeria requires a strong technological infrastructure, effective partnerships, and a commitment to customer satisfaction. By addressing logistical challenges and providing a convenient and reliable service, such a business can tap into the growing demand for food delivery in Nigeria's dynamic and urbanised market.

37. FROZEN FOOD SALES

Frozen food sales present a dual benefit by addressing both food security concerns and providing a viable business opportunity.

From a food security perspective, frozen foods offer a reliable means of preserving perishable items, reducing food waste, and ensuring a stable food supply. The extended shelf life of frozen foods allows for better distribution and storage, contributing to more efficient food management systems. This can be particularly crucial in regions where seasonal variations impact fresh produce availability.

As a business opportunity, the demand for convenient and time-saving food options is on the rise globally. Frozen food sales tap into this market trend, offering consumers a quick and easy solution for meal preparation. Entrepreneurs in this industry can benefit from the growing consumer interest in healthy and diverse frozen food options.

However, success in this venture requires careful consideration of logistical challenges, maintaining a reliable cold chain, and adapting to local preferences. Entrepreneurs should also explore technological advancements to enhance food preservation methods and stay competitive in the dynamic market.

Frozen food sales not only contribute to addressing food security concerns but also offer a lucrative business opportunity that aligns with changing consumer lifestyles and preferences.

38. SOFTWARE DEVELOPMENT

Software development is an excellent way to harness the energetic young population's addiction to technology and transform it into a profitable business venture. With the rising reliance on digital solutions, there is a growing demand for innovative software across various industries.

- *Youthful Expertise:*

The younger generation often has a natural affinity for technology, making them well-suited for software development. Their fresh perspectives and familiarity with the latest trends can lead to the creation of cutting-edge and market-relevant applications.

- *Entrepreneurial Spirit:*

Many young individuals possess an entrepreneurial spirit, making them inclined to start their own software development ventures. This can lead to the creation of startups that contribute to job creation and economic growth.

- *Global Market Reach:*

Software products have the potential for a global market reach. Young entrepreneurs can develop applications, websites, or software services that cater to an international audience, thereby expanding their business horizons.

- *Innovation and Creativity:*

The youthful population tends to be more innovative and creative. This mindset can drive the development of unique software solutions that stand out in the competitive market and attract users and customers.

- *Adaptability to Trends:*

The tech-savvy youth is quick to adapt to new trends and emerging technologies. This adaptability ensures that their software products stay relevant and up-to-date with the evolving tech landscape.

- *Problem-Solving Solutions:*

Software development provides an avenue to address societal challenges. Young entrepreneurs can focus on developing solutions that tackle specific problems, contributing to social impact while building a successful business.

- *Tech Ecosystem Collaboration:*

Engaging with the broader tech ecosystem, including incubators, accelerators, and networking events, can provide young developers with valuable resources, mentorship, and opportunities to scale their ventures.

However, aspiring entrepreneurs must understand the competitive nature of the software industry, stay updated with technological advancements, and prioritise user experience to ensure the success and sustainability of their ventures.

39. IT CONSULTING

IT consulting serves as a powerful tool for wealth creation for both individuals and businesses by leveraging expertise in information technology to provide valuable services. Here's how:

1. *Specialised Knowledge:* IT consultants possess specialised knowledge in various areas such as cybersecurity, software development, and system integration. This expertise is in

high demand, allowing consultants to offer solutions that businesses may not have in-house.

2. *Cost Efficiency:* Businesses can benefit from IT consulting by accessing specialised skills without the long-term costs associated with hiring full-time experts. This cost efficiency is attractive to companies looking to optimise their budgets.

3. *Strategic Guidance:* IT consultants provide strategic guidance to businesses, helping them align their technology investments with overall business objectives. This ensures that IT resources are used effectively to drive growth and efficiency.

4. *Problem Solving:* Consultants excel at problem-solving. They analyse challenges, propose effective solutions, and implement strategies to enhance business processes, ultimately increasing productivity and profitability.

5. *Adaptability to Change:* In the rapidly evolving IT landscape, consultants are adept at staying ahead of technological changes. This adaptability allows businesses to navigate shifts in the industry, ensuring they remain competitive.

6. *Customisation and Scalability:* IT consultants tailor solutions to meet the specific needs of their clients. This customisation ensures that businesses receive services aligned with their unique requirements. Additionally, consultants can scale their services as a business grows.

7. *Risk Mitigation:* Businesses can mitigate risks associated with technology implementations by leveraging the expertise of IT consultants. This proactive approach helps prevent potential issues and ensures the smooth operation of IT systems.

8. *Entrepreneurial Opportunities:* Individuals can build successful consulting businesses by offering services such as project

management, software development, or cybersecurity. This entrepreneurial avenue allows skilled professionals to create wealth through their expertise.

9. *Global Reach:* IT consulting often transcends geographical boundaries. Consultants can provide services remotely, opening up opportunities to work with clients globally and expanding their market reach.

IT consulting is a veritable tool for wealth creation. It offers businesses access to expertise, cost-efficient solutions, and strategic guidance. For individuals, it provides a pathway to entrepreneurship and financial success through the delivery of valuable IT services.

40. COMPUTER TRAINING CENTRE

Establishing a computer training centre is a highly relevant and impactful business venture in the current age and civilisation, particularly in the context of the Nigerian economy. This initiative addresses the urgent need for digitisation and technology skills development, contributing significantly to the nation's economic growth.

1. *Skill Development for the Digital Economy:* A computer training centre plays a pivotal role in equipping individuals with essential digital skills. As the Nigerian economy increasingly embraces technology, there is a growing demand for a digitally skilled workforce. Offering training programmes in areas like programming, digital marketing, and data analysis prepares individuals to meet the requirements of the evolving job market.
2. *Job Creation and Employability:* By providing comprehensive computer education, training centres contribute to job creation and enhanced employability. Graduates equipped

with relevant digital skills become valuable assets to businesses seeking to thrive in the digital age. This, in turn, addresses unemployment challenges and promotes economic empowerment.

3. *Empowering Entrepreneurs:* Computer training benefits aspiring entrepreneurs by providing them with the technical know-how needed to establish and manage digital businesses. This empowerment fosters innovation and the creation of startups, further diversifying the economy and fostering entrepreneurship.

4. *Meeting Industry Needs:* A computer training centre can tailor its programmes to address specific industry needs. For example, focusing on software development, cybersecurity, or digital marketing aligns training with the demands of various sectors, ensuring that graduates are well-prepared to contribute meaningfully to the workforce.

5. *Digital Inclusion:* Establishing training centres promotes digital inclusion by making technology education accessible to a broader demographic. This is particularly crucial in bridging the digital divide, ensuring that individuals from diverse backgrounds have the opportunity to participate in the digital economy.

6. *Supporting Government Initiatives:* Many governments, including Nigeria, are actively promoting digitisation and technological advancements. A computer training centre aligns with and supports these initiatives by preparing a workforce that can actively contribute to the government's vision for a digitally transformed economy.

7. *Continuous Learning Culture:* The digital landscape is dynamic, and a training centre fosters a culture of continuous learning. This ensures that individuals stay updated with the

latest technologies and trends, contributing to a workforce that is adaptable and responsive to industry changes.

In summary, a computer training centre serves as a catalyst for positive change in the Nigerian economy by addressing the pressing need for digitisation. Through skill development, job creation, and entrepreneurial empowerment, this business venture actively contributes to shaping a workforce ready to propel the nation into the digital era.

41. DIGITAL MARKETING AGENCY

In Nigeria's current economic state, a Digital Marketing Agency can be a formidable business due to the increasing adoption of online platforms and the growing importance of digital presence for businesses. As more companies recognise the need to establish a strong online footprint, digital marketing becomes crucial for reaching a wider audience and driving sales.

1. *Online Presence Demand:* Businesses are realising the significance of having a robust online presence. A digital marketing agency can help them navigate the digital landscape, optimise their websites, and effectively engage with their target audience.
2. *E-commerce Growth:* With the rise of e-commerce, businesses are seeking effective ways to market their products online. A digital marketing agency can play a pivotal role in creating and implementing strategies to boost online sales.
3. *Social Media Influence:* Social media platforms are powerful marketing tools in Nigeria. A digital marketing agency can leverage these platforms to enhance brand visibility, engage with the audience, and generate leads.
4. *Youthful Population:* Nigeria has a large youthful population that is highly active online. This demographic is more likely

to engage with digital content, making digital marketing a potent tool for reaching and influencing potential customers.

5. *Data Analytics Advantage:* Digital marketing allows for precise tracking and analysis of campaigns. Agencies can use data analytics to measure the success of marketing efforts, optimise strategies, and provide clients with measurable ROI.
6. *Cost-Effective Marketing:* Compared to traditional advertising, digital marketing can be more cost-effective, making it an attractive option for businesses looking to maximise their budget in challenging economic conditions.
7. *Remote Work Opportunities*: The digital nature of the business allows for remote work, enabling agencies to tap into a diverse pool of talent and potentially reduce operational costs.

While the economic landscape may pose challenges, the shift towards digitalisation and the need for businesses to adapt to online platforms present ample opportunities for a well-positioned digital marketing agency in Nigeria.

42. GRAPHIC DESIGN SERVICES

Graphic design services can generate revenue for an entrepreneur in various ways and hold significant importance in the world of Internet marketing:

1. *Branding and Logo Design:* Entrepreneurs often require unique and memorable logos and branding materials. Graphic design services can create visually appealing brand elements, helping businesses establish a strong and recognisable identity.

2. *Social Media Content:* Engaging visual content is essential in Internet marketing. Graphic designers can craft eye-catching graphics for social media posts, advertisements, and other online marketing campaigns, enhancing a brand's online presence.

3. *Website Design:* A well-designed website is crucial for user experience and can impact a visitor's perception of a business. Entrepreneurs can offer website design services, ensuring clients have visually appealing and user-friendly online platforms.

4. *Marketing Collateral:* Graphic designers can create marketing collateral such as brochures, flyers, and banners. These materials play a key role in offline and online marketing efforts, helping convey messages effectively to the target audience.

5. *E-book and Infographic Design:* Entrepreneurs involved in content marketing can leverage graphic design services to create visually appealing e-books, infographics, and other content assets. This enhances the overall quality of content and improves audience engagement.

6. *Advertising Materials:* Entrepreneurs running online advertising campaigns need visually compelling ad creatives. Graphic design services can produce impactful visuals for digital advertisements, improving click-through rates and overall campaign effectiveness.

7. *Print Design Services:* While internet marketing is dominant, there is still a need for print materials in certain scenarios. Graphic designers can offer services for designing business cards, posters, and other print materials.

8. *Responsive Design for Mobile:* With the increasing use of mobile devices, entrepreneurs can provide graphic design

services that focus on creating responsive designs, ensuring that websites and content adapt seamlessly to various screen sizes.

Graphic design services generate revenue for entrepreneurs by addressing the visual aspects of brand communication. In the world of internet marketing, where visual content plays a crucial role, these services contribute significantly to capturing audience attention, conveying messages effectively, and enhancing the overall brand image online.

43. SOCIAL MEDIA MANAGEMENT

Social Media Management is the strategic administration of an individual's or a company's presence on social media platforms. It involves creating, curating, and scheduling content, engaging with the audience, analysing performance metrics, and implementing strategies to enhance online visibility and reputation.

Making Tangible Money as a Social Media Management Business:

1. *Client Services:* Entrepreneurs can offer social media management as a service to businesses and individuals. This includes creating content calendars, managing posts, and interacting with the audience on behalf of clients. Charging a monthly retainer fee or per-project basis can generate consistent revenue.
2. *Consulting and Training:* Entrepreneurs with expertise in social media can provide consulting services to businesses looking to improve their in-house social media efforts. Additionally, offering training sessions or workshops on social media best practices can be a lucrative revenue stream.

3. *Content Creation and Curation:* Entrepreneurs can specialise in creating high-quality content for social media, including graphics, videos, and written posts. Selling these content creation services to clients can be a profitable aspect of a social media management business.
4. *Paid Advertising Management:* Managing paid advertising campaigns on social media platforms is a valuable skill. Entrepreneurs can offer services to businesses looking to maximise the effectiveness of their paid social media promotions, earning a percentage of the advertising budget.
5. *Analytics and Reporting:* Providing detailed analytics and performance reports is crucial for clients to understand the impact of their social media efforts. Entrepreneurs can offer reporting services, showcasing the success and areas for improvement, and charge for these insights.
6. *Affiliate Marketing:* Entrepreneurs can integrate affiliate marketing into their social media strategy by promoting products or services and earning a commission for each sale generated through their referral links. This can be particularly effective if the entrepreneur has a substantial following.
7. *Social Media Audits:* Offering social media audits can be a one-time service or an entry point to ongoing management. Entrepreneurs can analyse a client's current social media presence, identify areas for improvement, and propose strategies for optimisation.
8. *Sponsored Content and Partnerships:* Entrepreneurs who are influencers or experts in social media management can collaborate with brands for sponsored content or partnerships. Brands pay for exposure to the entrepreneur's engaged audience.

By combining these revenue streams, entrepreneurs can create a sustainable business model in social media management. Building a strong reputation, staying updated on industry trends, and consistently delivering value to clients are key factors in the success of such a venture.

44. E-COMMERCE PLATFORM

E-commerce Platforms:

E-commerce platforms in Nigeria, as elsewhere, are digital solutions that enable online buying and selling of goods and services. These platforms provide a virtual marketplace for businesses to showcase products, manage transactions, and interact with customers over the Internet.

Examples of E-commerce Platforms in Nigeria:

1. *Jumia:* One of the largest e-commerce platforms in Nigeria, offering a wide range of products, including electronics, fashion, and household items.
2. *Konga:* This is another prominent Nigerian e-commerce platform with a diverse product catalogue covering electronics, fashion, beauty, and more.
3. *PayPorte:* A Nigerian e-commerce platform known for its trendy offerings, PayPorte specialises in fashion and lifestyle products.
4. *Slot.ng:* Slot is a popular e-commerce platform in Nigeria with both an online presence and physical stores; they focus on electronics and gadgets.
5. *DealDey:* This is a platform that provides deals and discounts on various products and services, catering to a broad range of consumer interests.

Making Money as an E-commerce Platform Entrepreneur:

1. *Niche Focus:* Identify a specific niche or market segment that is underserved. Creating an e-commerce platform tailored to a particular niche can attract a dedicated customer base.
2. *Dropshipping Model:* Entrepreneurs can build e-commerce platforms that leverage the dropshipping model. This involves partnering with suppliers who handle inventory and shipping, allowing the entrepreneur to focus on sales and marketing.
3. *Multi-Vendor Marketplace:* Create a platform that allows multiple sellers to list and sell their products. Generate revenue by charging sellers a commission on each sale or through subscription fees for premium services.
4. *Subscription-Based Services:* Offer subscription-based services or products on the platform. This can include curated subscription boxes, premium content access, or exclusive member benefits.
5. *Affiliate Marketing:* Implement affiliate marketing programmes within the e-commerce platform. Earn commissions by promoting other businesses' products or services on the platform.
6. *Digital Products and Services:* Focus on selling digital products or services, such as e-books, online courses, or software. These products often have lower overhead costs and can be highly profitable.
7. *Value-Added Services:* Integrate value-added services like express delivery, quality assurance, or customer support to distinguish the platform and attract businesses and customers.
8. *Mobile App Development:* Create a mobile app for the e-commerce platform, providing a convenient and

accessible way for users to browse and make purchases. Monetise through app downloads or in-app purchases.

9. *Ad Spaces and Partnerships:* Sell advertising spaces on the platform to businesses looking to promote their products or services. Additionally, explore partnerships with other businesses for cross-promotion and mutually beneficial collaborations.

10. *Payment Processing Fees:* If the platform facilitates transactions, entrepreneurs can charge a small percentage or a fixed fee for each transaction processed through the platform.

By combining these strategies and staying attuned to market trends, aspiring entrepreneurs can create and monetise successful e-commerce platforms in Nigeria. Providing a seamless user experience, understanding the local market, and adapting to consumer needs are key factors for sustained success in the e-commerce industry.

45. ONLINE CONTENT CREATION

Online Content Creation Business:

Online content creation as a business involves producing and sharing digital content across various online platforms to entertain, educate, or engage audiences. This content can take various forms, including videos, blogs, podcasts, and social media posts, and can be monetised through advertising, sponsorships, merchandise sales, and more.

Examples of Successful Online Content Creators in Nigeria:

1. *Mark Angel Comedy* (Mark Angel and Emmanuella): Renowned for their humorous skits, Mark Angel Comedy

has gained international recognition on YouTube, amassing millions of subscribers and views.

2. *Dimma Umeh* (Beauty and Lifestyle Blogger): Dimma Umeh is a successful beauty and lifestyle content creator known for her engaging YouTube videos and social media presence. She shares makeup tutorials, product reviews, and lifestyle content.

3. *David 'Davido' Adeleke* (Musician and Vlogger): Davido is a successful musician who has also ventured into vlogging. His YouTube channel, Davido Adeleke, showcases behind-the-scenes moments, travels, and glimpses into his daily life.

4. *Sisi Yemmie* (Food and Lifestyle Blogger): Sisi Yemmie is a popular Nigerian food and lifestyle blogger who shares recipes, family vlogs, and relatable content on her YouTube channel and blog.

Utilising Online Content Creation for Wealth Creation:

1. *Identify Your Niche:* Choose a niche that aligns with your interests, skills, and the needs of your target audience. Whether it's fashion, technology, beauty, or comedy, specialising in a specific area can help you build a dedicated audience.

2. *Consistent Quality Content:* Consistency is key in the online content creation business. Regularly produce high-quality, engaging content to keep your audience entertained and coming back for more.

3. *Leverage Multiple Platforms:* Diversify your presence across various online platforms such as YouTube, Instagram, TikTok, and podcasts. This broadens your reach and allows you to connect with different audiences.

4. *Monetisation Strategies:* Explore various monetisation avenues, including ad revenue, sponsorships, affiliate marketing, and merchandise sales. As your audience grows, these avenues can become substantial sources of income.
5. *Engage with Your Audience:* Building a community around your content is crucial. Engage with your audience through comments, social media, and live sessions. Understanding your audience's preferences helps in creating content that resonates.
6. *Collaborate and Network:* Collaborate with other content creators and businesses within your niche. Partnerships and collaborations can introduce your content to new audiences and open up additional revenue streams.
7. *Invest in Quality Equipment:* Invest in good-quality cameras, microphones, and editing software to enhance the production value of your content. Professional-looking and sounding content can attract a larger audience and potential sponsors.
8. *Stay Updated on Trends:* Stay informed about trends and changes in the digital landscape. Adapting to new platforms, formats, or content trends keeps your content fresh and relevant.

By implementing these strategies, young entrepreneurs can turn online content creation into a profitable venture. It requires dedication, creativity, and a keen understanding of your audience, but with persistence, many have successfully built sustainable businesses in this dynamic field.

46. REAL ESTATE AGENCY

Real Estate Agency as a Profitable Business for Young Nigerians:

Real Estate Agency is a lucrative business venture that has empowered many young Nigerians to generate significant income. The real estate sector in Nigeria has experienced substantial growth due to urbanisation, population expansion, and increasing demand for housing and commercial spaces. Here's how Real Estate Agency proves to be a profitable business for young entrepreneurs:

1. High Commission Earnings:

Real estate transactions involve substantial amounts of money. As an agent, earning a percentage commission on property sales or rentals can result in significant income, especially when dealing with high-value properties.

2. Growing Demand for Properties

Nigeria's growing population and urbanisation contribute to an increased demand for properties. Young entrepreneurs in the real estate agency business can capitalise on this demand by connecting buyers with suitable properties and earning commissions in the process.

3. Diverse Portfolio Opportunities

Real estate encompasses various sectors, including residential, commercial, and industrial properties. Young entrepreneurs can diversify their portfolios, catering to different client needs and expanding revenue streams.

4. Rentals and Leasing Opportunities:

Facilitating property rentals and leasing agreements is a consistent source of income for real estate agents. The demand for rental properties is high, especially in urban areas, providing ongoing revenue through lease agreements.

5. Property Development Collaborations:

Some young entrepreneurs venture into property development collaborations, partnering with developers to market and sell newly constructed properties. This approach can lead to shared profits and increased revenue streams.

6. Real Estate Technology Integration:

Leveraging technology, such as online property listings and virtual tours, allows young real estate agents to reach a broader audience. Embracing digital platforms can enhance visibility, attract clients, and streamline transactions.

7. Networking Opportunities:

Building a strong network within the real estate industry is crucial. Young entrepreneurs can establish connections with property developers, investors, and other professionals, creating opportunities for collaboration and referrals.

8. Government Policies and Investments:

Government initiatives and investments in real estate, such as housing schemes and urban development projects, can create additional opportunities for young entrepreneurs to participate in the real estate market and benefit from associated transactions.

9. Real Estate Education and Consultancy:

Young entrepreneurs can provide real estate education and consulting services, guiding clients through the property buying or selling process. Offering expertise in market trends, legalities, and investment strategies adds value to clients and can result in additional revenue.

10. Adaptability to Market Trends:

Staying informed about market trends, property values, and regulatory changes enables young real estate agents to adapt their strategies. Being proactive and innovative in response to market dynamics can contribute to long-term success.

Real Estate Agency has proven to be a profitable business for many young Nigerians. With a growing property market, diverse opportunities, and the potential for substantial commissions, young entrepreneurs can thrive in Nigeria's dynamic and evolving real estate landscape.

47. PROPERTY DEVELOPMENT

Property development in Nigeria presents a lucrative opportunity driven by the country's rapid urbanisation, population growth, and a rising demand for housing and commercial spaces. As cities expand, the need for well-planned and modern infrastructure becomes paramount.

The ideal candidates for property development are individuals or entities with financial capacity and a comprehensive understanding of the real estate market. This includes entrepreneurs, investors, and developers with a keen eye for opportunities and a willingness to navigate the industry's complexities.

The financial requirements for property development in Nigeria can be substantial. Initial capital is needed for land acquisition, feasibility studies, and obtaining necessary permits. Construction costs, which can vary depending on the project scale and location, constitute a significant portion of the budget. Additionally, marketing and sales efforts require additional funding to attract potential buyers or tenants.

Given the substantial capital involved, individuals might need to explore various financing options, such as bank loans, partnerships, or real estate crowdfunding. Successful property developers often leverage their financial acumen to secure favourable terms and manage risks effectively.

Moreover, an in-depth understanding of the local market dynamics, regulatory landscape, and potential challenges is crucial. Thorough market research helps developers identify high-demand areas and tailor their projects to meet specific needs, ensuring a higher likelihood of success.

48. SHORT-TERM ACCOMMODATION (e.g., Airbnb)

Short-term accommodation, exemplified by platforms like Airbnb, is gaining momentum as a powerful business opportunity for entrepreneurs in Nigeria. The increasing number of travellers, both domestic and international, coupled with a growing preference for unique and personalised stays, has fuelled the demand for short-term rentals.

Entrepreneurs in Nigeria are capitalising on this trend by listing properties on platforms like Airbnb, turning homes or spare rooms into lucrative income streams. This model provides a flexible and scalable business option, requiring lower initial investments compared to traditional real estate ventures.

The appeal of short-term accommodation lies in its adaptability to different property types, from apartments to vacation homes. Entrepreneurs can leverage their local knowledge to offer authentic experiences, attracting travellers seeking a more immersive stay.

However, success in this business requires attention to detail, hospitality skills, and effective marketing strategies. Providing excellent customer service, maintaining property standards, and understanding local regulations are essential components of a thriving short-term accommodation venture.

The rise of short-term accommodation in Nigeria offers entrepreneurs a dynamic and profitable business avenue. By capitalising on the demand for unique and flexible stays, savvy individuals can transform their properties into sought-after destinations while contributing to the country's growing tourism sector.

49. INTERIOR DESIGN SERVICES

Establishing an interior design services business in Nigeria is a promising venture, given the country's evolving real estate landscape and the increasing demand for aesthetically pleasing and functional spaces. Nigeria's growing middle class, coupled with a heightened appreciation for interior aesthetics, creates a favourable environment for entrepreneurs in this industry.

Entrepreneurs entering the interior design sector can tap into various opportunities, including residential, commercial, and hospitality projects. The desire for modern and well-designed living and working spaces has spurred a demand for professional interior designers who can enhance functionality while creating visually appealing environments.

Furthermore, the Nigerian market's diverse cultural influences provide a rich palette for creativity in interior design. Entrepreneurs can draw inspiration from traditional motifs, contemporary trends, and global styles, allowing for a unique and customised approach to each project.

Effective marketing and networking are crucial in establishing a foothold in the interior design industry. Collaborating with real estate developers, architects, and local artisans can help entrepreneurs build a comprehensive network, expanding their reach and client base.

Given the competitive nature of the market, staying updated on design trends, utilising digital platforms for marketing, and offering top-notch customer service are key to success. Additionally, providing sustainable and eco-friendly design solutions aligns with the global shift towards more responsible and mindful living.

50. HOME RENOVATION SERVICES

Embarking on a home renovation service in Nigeria holds significant promise due to several factors that contribute to a thriving market. As the country experiences urbanisation, a rising middle class, and an increasing focus on property improvement, the demand for quality home renovation services is on the upswing.

Entrepreneurs in this sector have the opportunity to cater to a diverse range of needs, from basic repairs to comprehensive remodelling projects. Nigerian homeowners, recognising the value of enhancing their living spaces, are increasingly seeking professional services to revitalise and modernise their homes.

The potential for great returns in the home renovation business is amplified by the country's ageing housing stock, which often requires maintenance and upgrades. Entrepreneurs can capitalise on this by offering specialised services such as kitchen and bathroom renovations, electrical and plumbing upgrades, and energy-efficient solutions.

Effective marketing strategies, including showcasing before-and-after transformations, can attract homeowners looking to elevate their living spaces. Establishing a strong online presence, leveraging social media, and creating partnerships with real estate agents can contribute to business visibility and client acquisition.

Providing transparent cost estimates, adhering to timelines, and maintaining high-quality workmanship are essential for building a positive reputation and securing repeat business. Additionally, incorporating eco-friendly practices and materials aligns with the growing global emphasis on sustainability, appealing to environmentally conscious consumers.

51. LANDSCAPE DESIGN AND MAINTENANCE

Landscape Design and Maintenance businesses involve planning, designing, and maintaining outdoor spaces to enhance their aesthetic appeal, functionality, and sustainability. This encompasses elements such as plant selection, hardscape features, irrigation systems, and ongoing care to create visually pleasing and well-manicured environments.

In the modern Nigerian economy, a Landscape Design and Maintenance business is relevant to wealth creation for several reasons. Firstly, the country's urbanisation and increasing focus on real estate development has led to a growing demand for landscaped spaces around residential, commercial, and public areas. This creates opportunities for entrepreneurs to offer their expertise in designing and maintaining visually appealing outdoor environments.

Secondly, as people's appreciation for outdoor living spaces grows, there is a heightened desire to invest in properties with well-designed and well-maintained landscapes. Homeowners, real estate developers, and businesses recognise the value that a professionally landscaped environment adds to the overall aesthetic and market appeal of their properties.

Additionally, the emphasis on environmental sustainability and green practices aligns with the services provided by landscape design and maintenance businesses. Offering eco-friendly solutions, such as water-efficient irrigation systems and native plant selections, not only meets clients' evolving preferences but also positions the business favourably in the market.

Furthermore, well-maintained landscapes can significantly benefit the tourism and hospitality industries in Nigeria. Hotels, resorts, and public spaces that prioritise attractive outdoor areas can attract more visitors, contributing to overall economic growth.

52. PAINTING SERVICES

The Painting Services business in Nigeria has stood the test of time, remaining a resilient and profitable venture. Entrepreneurs in this industry can generate income through various avenues, including:

1. *Residential and Commercial Projects:* Offering painting services for homes, apartments, and commercial properties is a primary revenue stream. This includes both interior and exterior painting, catering to the diverse needs of property owners and businesses.
2. *New Construction and Renovation Projects:* As the real estate market grows, there is a continuous demand for painting services in new construction projects and renovations. Entrepreneurs can collaborate with developers and homeowners to provide quality paintwork that enhances the aesthetics of the spaces.
3. *Specialised Finishes and Techniques:* Providing specialised finishes, such as faux painting, texture painting, or mural work, allows entrepreneurs to differentiate their services

and cater to clients seeking unique and personalised design elements.

4. *Colour Consultation Services:* Offering colour consultation services to clients who may need guidance in choosing the right colour schemes for their spaces can add value to the business. This involves expertise in understanding colour psychology and design principles.

5. *Maintenance Contracts:* Establishing long-term relationships with clients through maintenance contracts can provide a steady stream of income. Regular touch-ups and maintenance work ensure the longevity of the paintwork, creating a reliable revenue source.

6. *Partnerships with Interior Designers and Contractors:* Collaborating with interior designers, architects, and contractors can lead to a consistent flow of projects. Building a network within the construction and design industry can result in referrals and ongoing partnerships.

7. *Branding and Marketing:* Creating a strong brand presence through effective marketing strategies, including online platforms and social media, can attract a broader customer base. Positive reviews and testimonials play a crucial role in securing new clients.

8. *Diversification of Services:* Expanding services to include related offerings such as wallpaper installation, epoxy flooring, or decorative finishes can broaden the business's scope and cater to a wider market.

In summary, a Painting Services business in Nigeria can be a lucrative venture for entrepreneurs who provide quality work, stay attuned to industry trends, and offer a range of services to meet diverse customer needs. Building a reputation for reliability, expertise, and creativity is key to long-term success in this age-old industry.

53. CLEANING SERVICES

The Cleaning Services business involves providing professional cleaning solutions for residential, commercial, and industrial spaces. Young entrepreneurs can generate substantial income from this business by implementing strategic approaches:

1. *Target Market Specialisation*: Identify and specialise in a specific niche within the cleaning industry, such as residential cleaning, office cleaning, post-construction cleanup, or specialised services like carpet or window cleaning. Focusing on a niche allows entrepreneurs to tailor their services and marketing efforts more effectively.
2. *Quality and Professionalism:* Providing high-quality cleaning services and maintaining a professional demeanour builds trust and satisfaction among clients. Consistently exceeding customer expectations often results in positive word-of-mouth referrals and repeat business.
3. *Technology Integration:* Leverage technology for scheduling, communication, and customer management. Implementing online booking systems, digital invoicing, and utilising social media for marketing can streamline operations and enhance visibility.
4. *Eco-Friendly Cleaning:* Respond to the growing demand for environmentally friendly practices by offering eco-friendly cleaning services. This can attract environmentally conscious clients and set the business apart from competitors.
5. *Subscription or Membership Models:* Introduce subscription-based or membership models, where clients can sign up for regular cleaning services. This ensures a steady stream

of income and establishes long-term relationships with customers.

6. *Employee Training and Background Checks:* Ensure a well-trained and trustworthy team by investing in employee training programmes and conducting thorough background checks. Clients are more likely to hire a cleaning service that values professionalism and reliability.

7. *Expand Service Offerings:* Consider expanding services to include additional offerings such as organising services, decluttering, or even property management. Diversifying services can attract a broader clientele and increase revenue streams.

8. *Referral programmes:* Implement referral programmes that incentivise existing clients to refer new business. Offering discounts or additional services for successful referrals can help expand the customer base.

9. *Online Marketing and Presence:* Establish a strong online presence through a professional website, social media platforms, and online advertising. Encourage satisfied clients to leave reviews and testimonials to enhance credibility.

10. *Localised Marketing:* Target local communities through door-to-door flyers, partnerships with local businesses, and community events. Personalised marketing efforts can create a strong presence in the target area.

In summary, young entrepreneurs can generate substantial income from a Cleaning Services business by combining quality service, strategic marketing, technology integration, and a customer-centric approach. Adapting to industry trends and consistently delivering exceptional results contribute to long-term success in the cleaning services sector.

54. PLUMBING SERVICES

Plumbing services present a lucrative business opportunity for young Nigerians due to increasing urbanisation and construction projects. The growing demand for housing and infrastructure creates a consistent need for skilled plumbers. Moreover, as technology advances, there is a rising demand for modern plumbing solutions, offering entrepreneurs the chance to specialise in innovative, efficient systems. By providing reliable and quality services, young Nigerians can tap into a market with sustained growth potential, contributing to both personal success and community development.

55. ELECTRICAL SERVICES

Establishing an electrical services business can be a profitable venture for young Nigerians for a variety of reasons. With the country's expanding population and ongoing urbanisation, there is a continuous demand for residential, commercial, and industrial electrical installations. The increasing number of construction projects and the need for regular maintenance create a consistent market for skilled electricians.

Furthermore, as technology evolves, there is a growing demand for expertise in renewable energy solutions and smart home systems. Young entrepreneurs can capitalise on these trends, positioning themselves as specialists in sustainable and cutting-edge electrical services.

Building a reputation for reliability, safety, and compliance with industry standards is crucial for success. Offering transparent pricing, excellent customer service, and keeping up with industry certifications can set a young electrical services business apart from competitors.

Moreover, with the government's focus on improving power infrastructure, young entrepreneurs in Nigeria can explore opportunities in collaboration with local authorities or participate in government projects.

In summary, the electrical services sector presents a reliable business opportunity for young Nigerians due to the continuous demand for electrical expertise in a developing economy, coupled with emerging trends in technology and sustainability.

56. MINI ELECTRIC POWER GENERATION AND DISTRIBUTION.

Establishing a mini electric power generation and distribution business in rural and suburban areas of Nigeria holds significant profit potential due to the persistent challenges in electric power access. These regions often face unreliable or no connection to the national grid, creating a demand for alternative power solutions.

Entrepreneurs can tap into this market by investing in mini power generation systems, such as solar or small-scale hydroelectric plants. These localised solutions cater to the specific energy needs of communities, providing a reliable and sustainable source of electricity. The potential for profitability arises from the following factors:

1. *Unmet Demand*: Many rural and suburban areas lack consistent access to electricity, leading to a high demand for reliable power sources. Entrepreneurs addressing this gap can capture a substantial market share.
2. *Government Initiatives:* Government incentives and initiatives aimed at promoting renewable energy projects provide additional support for entrepreneurs entering the mini-power generation sector. This can include subsidies, tax breaks, or partnerships with governmental agencies.

3. *Community Development:* Beyond profitability, entrepreneurs can contribute to community development by enhancing the quality of life in these areas. Access to electricity can stimulate economic activities, improve healthcare, and facilitate education, fostering a positive social impact.
4. *Diversification of Services:* Entrepreneurs can diversify their offerings by not only providing power generation but also establishing distribution networks. This could involve setting up mini-grids that serve multiple households and businesses, creating a sustainable revenue stream.
5. *Technology Integration:* Leveraging advancements in energy storage and management technologies allows entrepreneurs to optimise power distribution systems. This ensures efficient use of resources and enhances the overall reliability of the service.

To maximise profits, entrepreneurs should conduct thorough market research, engage with local communities, and establish scalable and sustainable business models. By addressing the pressing need for electricity in rural and suburban areas, a mini electric power generation and distribution business can not only generate substantial profits but also contribute to the broader development goals of the region.

57. PHARMACY OR DRUG STORE

The Pharmacy or drugstore business has indeed been a longstanding venture, and its relevance has only increased as public health facilities face challenges. The deteriorating state of public health facilities often leads people to turn to local pharmacies or drug stores for accessible healthcare solutions. Here's a discussion on the matter:

1. *Increased Demand:* With public health facilities facing challenges such as long wait times, inadequate resources, and sometimes limited accessibility, more individuals rely on local pharmacies for immediate access to essential medications and health advice. This surge in demand creates a significant business opportunity for entrepreneurs in the pharmacy sector.
2. *Community Health Support:* Pharmacies play a crucial role in supporting community health. Beyond providing medications, they offer valuable advice on over-the-counter remedies, health supplements, and preventive measures. Entrepreneurs in this business can actively contribute to public health by ensuring their staff is well-informed and capable of offering sound healthcare guidance.
3. *Accessibility and Convenience:* The convenience of having a local pharmacy nearby becomes essential when public health facilities face challenges. Entrepreneurs can capitalise on this need for accessibility, strategically locating their pharmacies to serve communities where healthcare access is limited.
4. *Diversification of Services:* Beyond traditional drug dispensing, pharmacies can diversify their services. Offering health screenings and vaccinations and collaborating with healthcare professionals can further enhance the role of the pharmacy as a community health hub. This not only benefits the business but also contributes to public health improvement.
5. *Technology Integration:* Entrepreneurs can leverage technology to streamline operations and enhance customer experience. Online ordering, prescription refills, and telepharmacy services can provide added convenience for customers,

especially in areas where physical access might be a challenge.

6. *Health Education Initiatives:* Entrepreneurs can engage in community health education initiatives. Hosting workshops and seminars or distributing informative materials about common health issues can position the pharmacy as a trusted source of health information.

The pharmacy or drugstore business has become increasingly vital as public health facilities face challenges. Entrepreneurs entering this sector not only have the opportunity for a profitable business but also play a crucial role in addressing the healthcare needs of their communities, contributing to improved public health outcomes.

58. FITNESS CENTRE OR GYM

Establishing a Fitness Centre or Gym in an elite environment can indeed be a lucrative and sustainable venture, given the growing emphasis on health and wellness. Here's a discussion of why this business can be a sure money-making opportunity:

1. *Health-Conscious Elite Population:* The elite demographic often places a high priority on health and fitness. Establishing a gym in such an environment caters to individuals who are willing to invest in their well-being, leading to a consistent customer base.

2. *Premium Services and Amenities:* To cater to the elite market, entrepreneurs can offer premium services and amenities such as personalised training programmes, state-of-the-art equipment, spa facilities, and exclusive classes. These added features not only attract clients but also justify higher membership fees.

3. *Holistic Wellness Approach:* Entrepreneurs can incorporate a holistic wellness approach to go beyond traditional gym services. This might include nutrition counselling, wellness retreats, and partnerships with healthcare professionals, creating a comprehensive health and fitness experience.

4. *Networking Opportunities*: Elite environments often foster networking and social connections. Establishing a gym in such an area provides an opportunity for individuals to meet like-minded individuals, creating a community around the fitness centre. This sense of community can enhance customer retention and attract new members through referrals.

5. *Corporate Partnerships:* Entrepreneurs can explore partnerships with local businesses or corporate entities to offer fitness programmes to their employees. Corporate wellness programmes are increasingly popular, and a gym in an elite environment can position itself as an ideal partner for such initiatives.

6. *Technology Integration:* Incorporating technology-driven fitness solutions, such as virtual classes, fitness apps, and wearable technology integration, can appeal to the tech-savvy elite population. Offering a seamless and modern fitness experience enhances the overall attractiveness of the gym.

7. *Exclusive Memberships:* Creating tiers of memberships with exclusive benefits can appeal to the elite market. This might include priority access to classes, personalised training sessions, or reserved workout spaces, providing added value for higher-tier memberships.

A Fitness Centre or Gym in an elite environment presents a sure money-making venture due to the target market's health-conscious mindset and willingness to invest in premium fitness services. By offering exclusive amenities, personalised experiences, and embracing a holistic wellness approach, entrepreneurs can position their gym as a sought-after destination for the elite demographic, ensuring long-term success and profitability.

59. HEALTHCARE CONSULTING

Starting a Healthcare Consulting business in Nigeria holds significant profit potential due to the rapidly growing population that outpaces the available healthcare services. Here's a comprehensive discussion of why this business can be profitable:

1. *High Demand for Quality Healthcare:* Nigeria's expanding population has led to increased demand for quality healthcare services. Healthcare consulting businesses can capitalise on this by offering expertise to healthcare providers, guiding them in improving their services, and ensuring compliance with industry standards.
2. *Infrastructure and System Improvement:* The healthcare sector in Nigeria faces challenges related to infrastructure and systems. A consulting business can thrive by assisting healthcare facilities in optimising their operations, implementing efficient management systems, and upgrading infrastructure to meet the rising demand.
3. *Regulatory Compliance and Quality Assurance:* As the healthcare industry becomes more regulated, consulting services that focus on ensuring regulatory compliance and maintaining quality standards are in high demand. Healthcare providers seek assistance in navigating complex regulations, which presents a lucrative market for consulting businesses.
4. *Telemedicine and Technological Integration:* The global trend towards telemedicine and technology-driven healthcare solutions is also relevant in Nigeria. Consulting firms can

guide healthcare organisations in adopting and integrating technology to enhance patient care, streamline processes, and improve overall efficiency.

5. *Training and Capacity Building:* To meet the growing demands, skilled healthcare professionals are needed. Healthcare consulting businesses can offer training programmes and capacity-building services to address the shortage of qualified personnel, providing a valuable service to both healthcare providers and aspiring professionals.
6. *Public-Private Partnerships:* The government's focus on improving healthcare services opens up opportunities for public-private partnerships. Healthcare consulting firms can play a pivotal role in facilitating collaborations between the public and private sectors, leveraging expertise to enhance service delivery.
7. *Data Management and Analytics:* The healthcare sector generates vast amounts of data, and consulting businesses specialising in data management and analytics can help healthcare providers harness the power of data for informed decision-making, improved patient outcomes, and operational efficiency.
8. *Health Insurance Advisory:* With the growing awareness of the importance of health insurance, consulting firms can provide advisory services to individuals and businesses, guiding them in selecting appropriate health insurance plans and navigating the complexities of the healthcare financing landscape.

Healthcare consulting businesses in Nigeria can be highly profitable due to the increasing population, which puts pressure on existing healthcare services. By addressing the challenges in the healthcare sector, providing strategic guidance, and leveraging opportunities for improvement, consulting firms can play a pivotal role in shaping a more robust and efficient healthcare system while enjoying significant financial success.

60. NUTRITIONAL COUNSELLING

Nutritional Counselling Definition:

Nutritional counselling is a specialised service provided by trained professionals, such as dietitians or nutritionists, to help individuals optimise their diet and make informed choices regarding their nutritional intake. It involves personalised guidance on dietary habits, meal planning, and lifestyle adjustments tailored to meet specific health goals, manage medical conditions, or enhance overall well-being.

Why Nutritional Counselling is a Prospective Business:

1. *Rising Diet Consciousness:* As diet consciousness spreads rapidly among the population, people are becoming more aware of the impact of nutrition on their health. This increased awareness creates a demand for expert guidance, making nutritional counselling a business with substantial growth prospects.
2. *Health and Wellness Trend:* The global trend towards health and wellness has fueled interest in nutrition as a fundamental component of a healthy lifestyle. Nutritional counselling aligns with this trend, offering individuals the knowledge and support they need to make healthier food choices.
3. *Preventive Healthcare Focus:* With a growing emphasis on preventive healthcare, individuals are proactively seeking ways to improve their health through lifestyle changes, including dietary modifications. Nutritional counselling

addresses this shift by providing preventive strategies to promote long-term well-being.

4. *Individualised Approach:* Nutritional counselling offers personalised advice based on individual needs, health conditions, and goals. The emphasis on customisation appeals to clients seeking tailored solutions, contributing to the business's attractiveness.

5. *Chronic Disease Management:* As the prevalence of chronic diseases like obesity, diabetes, and cardiovascular issues increases, there is a heightened demand for nutritional counselling services. Professionals in this field can play a crucial role in managing and preventing these health conditions through diet modification.

6. *Corporate Wellness programmes:* Businesses are recognising the importance of employee well-being. Nutritional counselling services can be integrated into corporate wellness programmes, providing organisations with a valuable resource to support the health and productivity of their workforce.

7. *Online Accessibility:* The digital age has facilitated online accessibility to nutritional counselling services. This broadens the business's reach, allowing professionals to offer virtual consultations and reach a wider audience.

8. *Media Influence and Social Media:* Influencers, celebrities, and health advocates use social media platforms to promote healthy lifestyles, including dietary choices. This heightened exposure further fuels the interest in nutritional counselling as individuals seek professional guidance inspired by online influencers.

The surge in diet consciousness, coupled with the broader health and wellness trend, positions nutritional counselling as a business with immense prospects. The individualised approach, focus on preventive healthcare, and adaptability to online platforms contribute to the attractiveness of this business in meeting the evolving needs of a health-conscious population.

61. MEDICAL LABORATORY

The evolution of Medical Laboratories in Nigeria reflects a shift from large establishments to more agile and mobile setups, driven by advancements in technology, changes in healthcare practices, and the demand for convenient and accessible diagnostic services. Here's a discussion in the context of the Nigerian healthcare system:

1. Transition to Test Kits:

The adoption of test kits has transformed diagnostic practices. These kits, often more portable and user-friendly, allow for quicker and on-the-spot testing. This is particularly beneficial in Nigeria, where remote areas may face challenges accessing traditional laboratory facilities.

2. Increased Accessibility:

Mobile medical laboratories cater to the need for increased accessibility, especially in underserved or rural areas with limited healthcare infrastructure. Individuals and communities can benefit from diagnostic services without the need to travel long distances to centralised facilities.

3. Technological Advancements:

The integration of technology in diagnostics has allowed for more efficient and accurate testing processes. Portable devices and automated systems contribute to the effectiveness of both traditional and mobile laboratories, enhancing the overall quality of diagnostic services in Nigeria.

4. Point-of-Care Testing:

The concept of point-of-care testing has gained prominence, enabling rapid and real-time results. This is particularly crucial in emergencies and for conditions that require immediate attention, aligning with the dynamic healthcare needs in Nigeria.

5. Entrepreneurial Opportunities:

The transition to mobile medical laboratories creates entrepreneurial opportunities for individuals to establish their diagnostic services. This flexibility allows for cost-effective setups, making it feasible for entrepreneurs to address specific healthcare gaps in their communities.

6. Public Health Impact:

Mobile medical laboratories contribute to public health by facilitating early diagnosis and intervention. This is vital in managing and controlling the spread of diseases, particularly in a country as populous as Nigeria.

7. Challenges and Regulation:

While the shift towards mobile laboratories brings advantages, it also poses challenges, such as ensuring the quality and accuracy of results. Regulatory frameworks become crucial to maintain standards and safeguard public health.

8. Collaboration with Healthcare Providers:

Mobile medical laboratories can collaborate with healthcare providers and community health workers to extend their reach.

This collaborative approach enhances the integration of diagnostic services into broader healthcare initiatives.

9. Community Health Screenings:

Mobile laboratories can play a pivotal role in community health screenings, offering services ranging from basic health checks to more specialised diagnostic tests. This proactive approach aligns with preventive healthcare strategies.

62. HOME HEALTHCARE SERVICES

Home Healthcare Services Definition:

Home healthcare services involve delivering medical and non-medical care to individuals in the comfort of their homes. These services are administered by healthcare professionals, including doctors, nurses, and other trained caregivers, to address a variety of healthcare needs, from medical treatments to assistance with daily activities.

Entrepreneurial Opportunities for Young Doctors and Nurses in Nigeria:

1. Increasing ageing Population:

Nigeria, like many countries, is experiencing an increase in its ageing population. Home healthcare services cater to the healthcare needs of elderly individuals who prefer to receive medical attention in the familiar environment of their homes. Young doctors and nurses can tap into this growing market.

2. Chronic Disease Management:

The prevalence of chronic diseases is on the rise in Nigeria. Home healthcare services provide an opportunity for young healthcare professionals to specialise in chronic disease management, offering personalised care plans and monitoring to patients with conditions such as diabetes, hypertension, and respiratory disorders.

3. Post-Hospitalisation Care:

Many patients require continued care after being discharged from hospitals. Home healthcare services bridge the gap between hospital and home, ensuring a smooth transition and reducing the likelihood of readmissions. Young doctors and nurses can establish services that focus on post-hospitalisation care.

4. Technological Integration:

Leveraging technology in home healthcare services can enhance the efficiency and effectiveness of care. Young healthcare entrepreneurs can incorporate telehealth solutions, remote monitoring devices, and mobile applications to provide comprehensive and technologically advanced services.

5. Personalised and Holistic Care:

Home healthcare allows for personalised and holistic care tailored to the unique needs of each patient. Young doctors and nurses can create niche services that focus on delivering individualised care plans, fostering a more patient-centred approach to healthcare.

6. Community Health Outreach:

Home healthcare services enable healthcare professionals to engage in community health outreach. By providing services directly within communities, young doctors and nurses can contribute to improving healthcare access in both urban and rural areas.

7. Flexible Entrepreneurial Models:

Home healthcare services can be structured in various entrepreneurial models, including establishing private practices, collaborating with existing healthcare organisations, or creating startups that focus on specific healthcare niches. This flexibility allows young professionals to tailor their entrepreneurial ventures to their preferences and expertise.

8. Government and NGO Collaborations:

Collaboration with government health initiatives and non-governmental organisations (NGOs) can open doors for young healthcare entrepreneurs. By aligning their services with broader healthcare goals, entrepreneurs can contribute to public health efforts while building successful businesses.

9. Preventive Healthcare programmes:

Home healthcare services can extend beyond treatment to include preventive healthcare programmes. Young doctors and nurses can design initiatives that focus on health education, screenings, and early detection of health issues within the home setting.

Home healthcare services present substantial entrepreneurial opportunities for young doctors and nurses in Nigeria. By addressing the evolving healthcare needs of the population and leveraging innovative approaches, these professionals can establish successful ventures that not only contribute to their own careers but also enhance the overall healthcare landscape in the country.

63. HERBAL MEDICINE PRODUCTION

The utilisation of herbal and alternative medicines, particularly in their crude forms, presents a unique opportunity in the healthcare business, representing a new goldmine. Here's a discussion of why this trend is gaining prominence and creating lucrative prospects:

1. Growing Demand for Natural Therapies:

There is a global shift towards natural and holistic healthcare approaches. Consumers are increasingly seeking alternatives to conventional medicines, leading to a surge in the demand for herbal remedies in their pure, unprocessed forms.

2. Cultural and Traditional Roots:

Many regions, including Nigeria, have rich cultural and traditional medicinal practices that involve the use of herbal remedies. The resurgence of interest in these traditional healing methods contributes to the newfound popularity of herbal medicines in their crude form.

3. Holistic Wellness Trend:

The emphasis on holistic wellness has led to a broader acceptance of herbal remedies, viewed as a part of a comprehensive approach to health. This trend extends beyond treating specific ailments, focusing on overall well-being and prevention.

4. Diverse Medicinal Plants:

Nigeria boasts a rich biodiversity of medicinal plants with therapeutic properties. Entrepreneurs in the healthcare business can tap into this wealth of resources by exploring the identification, cultivation, and sustainable harvesting of these plants for herbal remedies.

5. Innovation in Processing Techniques:

The challenge of mass production, distribution, and preservation of herbal remedies in crude form has prompted innovation in processing techniques. Entrepreneurs can develop methods for standardising, packaging, and preserving herbal products while retaining their efficacy.

6. Regulatory Framework and Quality Assurance:

Establishing a robust regulatory framework and ensuring quality assurance are critical in building trust in herbal products. Entrepreneurs can work towards standardising production processes, adhering to quality control measures, and obtaining necessary certifications for their herbal remedies.

7. Integration with Mainstream Healthcare:

The integration of herbal remedies into mainstream healthcare practices is gaining recognition. Entrepreneurs can explore partnerships with healthcare providers, offering herbal supplements as complementary options or exploring collaborative research initiatives to validate the efficacy of traditional herbal medicines.

8. Global Market Potential:

The global market for herbal and alternative medicines is expanding. Entrepreneurs can position their products to cater not only to local markets but also to the growing international demand for natural and plant-based remedies

9. Educational Initiatives:

Entrepreneurial opportunities lie in educating the public about the benefits and uses of herbal remedies. Establishing educational initiatives can help dispel myths, provide accurate information, and create awareness, contributing to the wider acceptance of herbal medicines.

10. Environmental Sustainability:

With an increasing focus on sustainability, entrepreneurs can engage in environmentally friendly practices. This includes promoting sustainable harvesting of medicinal plants, cultivating them in controlled environments, and adopting eco-friendly packaging methods.

In conclusion, the use of herbal remedies in their crude form presents a new goldmine in the healthcare business. Entrepreneurs can leverage the demand for natural therapies, integrate innovative processing techniques, navigate regulatory challenges, and contribute to the global shift towards holistic wellness, creating a profitable and sustainable niche in the healthcare industry.

64. VALUE ADDITION BUSINESS

Investing in value addition is crucial for young entrepreneurs, especially in traditional African contexts where the historical trend of selling unprocessed goods has prevailed. Here's a discussion on why adding value to goods is imperative for maximising profits and fostering economic development:

1. Increased Profit Margins:

Value-added products generally command higher prices in the market. By transforming raw materials into finished or processed goods, entrepreneurs can significantly increase profit margins, leading to greater financial returns on their investments.

2. Competitive Advantage:

In a globalised market, competition is intense. Value-added products often stand out, providing a competitive edge. Entrepreneurs can differentiate themselves by offering unique, high-quality goods that meet specific consumer needs, contributing to increased market share.

3. Job Creation and Economic Growth:

Value addition often involves more complex production processes, requiring skilled labour. By investing in value addition, entrepreneurs contribute to job creation, fostering economic growth and providing opportunities for individuals in their communities.

4. Enhanced Market Access:

Many international markets have stringent quality and safety standards. Value-added products are more likely to meet these standards, facilitating easier access to global markets. This opens up opportunities for young entrepreneurs to participate in international trade and expand their businesses.

5. Preservation of Cultural Heritage:

Value addition can be an avenue for preserving traditional practices and cultural heritage. Entrepreneurs can create products that showcase the unique cultural identity of their regions, attracting consumers interested in authentic and culturally rich offerings.

6. Risk Mitigation:

Selling unprocessed goods exposes entrepreneurs to market fluctuations and price volatility. Value addition can act as a risk mitigation strategy by diversifying the product range and reducing vulnerability to external economic factors.

7. Consumer Preferences and Trends:

Consumer preferences are evolving, with a growing demand for convenience, quality, and innovative products. Value-added goods can align with these changing trends, capturing the interest of consumers who seek more than basic commodities.

8. Technology Integration:

Embracing technology in the value-addition process can enhance efficiency and quality. Entrepreneurs can leverage technology to improve production processes, reduce waste, and optimise resource utilisation, contributing to sustainable and cost-effective operations.

9. Supply Chain Strengthening:

Adding value often involves building a more robust supply chain. Entrepreneurs can establish relationships with local farmers, producers, and suppliers, creating a network that supports their value-addition initiatives and fosters community collaboration.

10. Sustainability and Environmental Considerations:

Value addition can incorporate sustainable practices, minimising environmental impact. Entrepreneurs investing in environmentally friendly production methods align with global sustainability goals, appealing to conscious consumers and contributing to responsible business practices.

Young entrepreneurs in traditional African contexts are advised to recognise the immense benefits of investing in value addition. Beyond maximising profits, this approach contributes to economic development, job creation, and cultural preservation and aligns with evolving consumer preferences. By breaking away from the historical trend of selling unprocessed goods, entrepreneurs can build resilient businesses with a lasting impact on both local and international markets.

65. A DENTAL CLINIC BUSINESS

A Dental Clinic business, while often considered less popular than other healthcare ventures, is strategically crucial to the overall healthcare system. Here's a discussion of why investing in a Dental Clinic is a strategic and valuable undertaking:

1. Oral Health's Integral Role:

Oral health is an integral component of overall well-being. Dental issues can impact systemic health, leading to various health concerns if left untreated. A Dental Clinic contributes to preventive care and early intervention, reducing the burden on the broader healthcare system.

2. Preventive Focus:

Dental clinics play a significant role in preventive healthcare. Regular check-ups, cleanings, and education provided by dental professionals can help prevent common oral health issues, contributing to overall health promotion and reducing the need for more extensive medical interventions.

3. Community Health Improvement:

Dental health is crucial for community health improvement. A Dental Clinic addresses the specific oral health needs of the local population, promoting healthier lifestyles and contributing to the overall well-being of the community.

4. Specialised Expertise:

Dental professionals bring specialised expertise to the healthcare system. Dentists are trained to diagnose and treat various dental conditions, offering specialised services that complement the broader range of healthcare providers. This specialisation ensures comprehensive care for patients.

5. Pain Management and Quality of Life:

Dental issues, if neglected, can lead to severe pain and a significant reduction in the quality of life. Dental clinics provide timely interventions to manage pain, restore oral function, and enhance the overall well-being of individuals.

6. Contribution to Aesthetic and Psychological Health:

Beyond medical considerations, dental care contributes to aesthetic and psychological health. Dental procedures, such as cosmetic dentistry, can boost self-esteem and positively impact mental health, highlighting the holistic nature of oral healthcare.

7. Emergency Care and Trauma Management:

Dental clinics are equipped to handle emergency cases and trauma management related to oral health. Prompt attention to dental emergencies can prevent complications, ensuring that individuals receive timely and appropriate care.

8. Gateway to Early Detection of Systemic Issues:

Oral health professionals often have the opportunity to detect early signs of systemic health issues during routine dental examinations. This early detection can lead to timely referrals to other healthcare specialists, contributing to a more comprehensive approach to healthcare.

9. Contribution to Disease Prevention:

Periodontal diseases have been linked to various systemic conditions, including cardiovascular diseases and diabetes. Dental clinics contribute to disease prevention by addressing these connections and promoting oral health practices that can positively impact overall health.

10. Business Sustainability:

From a business perspective, a Dental Clinic can be sustainable due to the recurring nature of dental services. Regular check-ups, cleanings, and preventive care contribute to a steady stream of patients, ensuring a stable and reliable business model.

In conclusion, a Dental Clinic business is strategically crucial to the healthcare system due to its focus on preventive care, specialised expertise, contribution to community health improvement, and its role in overall well-being. The impact of oral health on systemic health underscores the importance of integrating dental care into the broader healthcare landscape.

66. OPTICAL CLINIC

The combination of harsh environmental factors and poor diets has significantly increased the prevalence of eye problems among Nigerians. Factors such as dust, pollution, and exposure to harsh sunlight contribute to various eye conditions, while inadequate nutrition can lead to deficiencies that impact ocular health. As a result, the demand for optical services and products has risen significantly, making the optical shop business a promising venture in today's economy.

Optical clinics play a crucial role in addressing the growing needs of individuals experiencing vision issues. These establishments provide access to essential eye care services, including vision tests, prescription glasses, contact lenses, and other vision aids. Moreover, they offer a wide range of products tailored to address specific eye conditions, such as specialised lenses for astigmatism or anti-glare coatings for computer users.

Optical clinics address existing eye problems and actively promote preventive care. They educate patients on the importance of regular eye examinations and offer guidance on maintaining optimal eye health through proper eyewear and lifestyle choices. Furthermore, advancements in technology have enabled optical clinics to offer cutting-edge solutions, such as digital eye strain relief lenses and blue light filtering coatings, catering to the evolving needs of patients in an increasingly digital world.

From a business perspective, the optical clinic presents lucrative opportunities for entrepreneurs. With the growing demand for eye care services, there is a steady stream of potential patients seeking solutions to their vision-related concerns. Moreover, as awareness of the importance of eye health continues to increase, patients are becoming more willing to invest in quality eye care products and services, driving revenue growth for optical businesses.

However, success in the optical clinic business requires more than just offering products and services; it demands a commitment to excellence in customer service, product quality, and professional expertise. Building trust and establishing a reputation for reliability and expertise are essential for long-term success in this competitive industry.

67. PRIVATE TUTORING

The education landscape in Nigeria is marked by several challenges, including a significant number of uneducated adults, concerns about the safety of children in boarding schools, and students' diverse learning abilities. In response to these challenges, private tutoring has emerged as a crucial service, offering tailored educational support to address the specific needs of individual learners. This dynamic presents a wealth of prospects for private tutors seeking to make a meaningful impact while building a successful business.

One of the primary drivers of private tutoring's appeal is its ability to provide personalised attention and targeted instruction. With large class sizes and limited resources in many educational settings, students with varying learning abilities often struggle to receive the individualised support they require. Private tutors fill this gap by offering one-on-one or small group sessions tailored to each student's unique learning style, pace, and areas of difficulty. This personalised approach not only enhances academic performance but also boosts students' confidence and motivation, fostering a more positive attitude towards learning.

Moreover, the flexibility inherent in private tutoring allows tutors to adapt their approach to meet the specific needs of their clients. Whether it's providing remedial support for struggling students, offering enrichment activities for high achievers, or preparing students for standardised tests and examinations, private tutors can tailor their services to align with the goals and aspirations of their students and their families. This versatility enables tutors to cater to a broad spectrum of educational needs, expanding their potential client base and business opportunities.

Additionally, the growing concern over the safety and quality of education in boarding schools has prompted many parents to seek alternative learning options for their children. Private tutoring offers a safe and controlled environment where students can receive personalised attention without the risks associated with residential schooling. This shift towards alternative educational solutions further amplifies the demand for private tutoring services, presenting tutors with a ripe market of parents eager to invest in their children's academic success and well-being.

Furthermore, the proliferation of technology has expanded the reach and accessibility of private tutoring, allowing tutors to offer their services online to students across geographic locations. This virtual format not only increases convenience for both tutors and students but also opens up new avenues for business growth and expansion. By leveraging online platforms and digital tools, tutors can reach a wider audience, differentiate their services, and diversify their revenue streams, tapping into the burgeoning market for online education.

Private tutoring represents a thriving business opportunity in Nigeria, driven by the need to address the challenges and shortcomings of the traditional education system. With its emphasis on personalised instruction, flexibility, and safety, private tutoring offers a compelling value proposition for parents and students alike. As the demand for quality education continues to rise, private tutors stand to benefit from a wealth of prospects, making it an attractive and rewarding venture for aspiring entrepreneurs in the education sector.

68. LANGUAGE SCHOOL

In Nigeria, where linguistic diversity is a defining characteristic, language barriers can present significant obstacles to the transfer of knowledge, technology, and values. Recognising the importance of bridging these barriers, the business of language schools holds considerable promise in the current economic landscape.

Language schools play a vital role in facilitating communication and cultural exchange by offering comprehensive language learning programmes tailored to the needs of individuals and organisations. In a globalised world where cross-cultural collaboration is increasingly essential for economic growth and innovation, proficiency in multiple languages enhances competitiveness and opens up new opportunities for businesses and individuals alike.

The demand for language skills is particularly pronounced in Nigeria's economic situation, which is characterised by a growing emphasis on diversification and international partnerships. As the country seeks to expand its presence in global markets and attract foreign investment, proficiency in languages such as English, French, Mandarin, and Arabic becomes increasingly valuable. Language schools can capitalise on this demand by offering specialised courses designed to equip students with the language skills needed to thrive in diverse professional settings.

Furthermore, the proliferation of technology and online learning platforms presents new avenues for language schools to reach a broader audience and adapt their offerings to the evolving needs of learners. By leveraging digital tools and multimedia resources, language schools can deliver immersive and interactive learning experiences that transcend geographical barriers, making language learning more accessible and engaging for students across Nigeria.

Moreover, the cultural exchange facilitated by language schools contributes to fostering mutual understanding and appreciation among individuals from different backgrounds. As Nigeria continues to navigate socio-political challenges and strive for national unity, initiatives that promote intercultural dialogue and empathy are crucial for fostering social cohesion and harmony.

From a business perspective, the language school sector offers entrepreneurs opportunities to capitalise on the growing demand for language learning services. By developing innovative curricula, leveraging technology to enhance learning outcomes, and forging strategic partnerships with businesses and educational institutions, language schools can position themselves for sustainable growth and profitability in the Nigerian market.

The business of language schools holds considerable promise in Nigeria's current economic landscape, where language barriers pose challenges to knowledge transfer and cultural exchange. By addressing the growing demand for language skills and fostering intercultural understanding, language schools play a vital role in driving economic development, promoting social cohesion, and positioning Nigeria for success in an increasingly interconnected world.

69. SKILL ACQUISITION CENTRE

Establishing a Skill Acquisition Centre can indeed be a profitable venture in today's reality, where the skill economy is highly valued. Here are some points to consider in discussing its profitability:

1. *High Demand:* With rapid technological advancements and evolving job markets, there's a growing demand for

individuals with specialised skills. A Skill Acquisition Centre can cater to this demand by offering training programmes in various in-demand fields such as digital marketing, coding, data analysis, graphic design, etc.

2. *Adaptability:* A well-designed Skill Acquisition Centre can quickly adapt to changing industry needs and trends. This adaptability ensures that the centre remains relevant and can continue to attract students seeking to acquire new skills or upgrade existing ones.

3. *Diversified Revenue Streams:* Beyond traditional classroom-based training, a Skill Acquisition Centre can diversify its revenue streams by offering online courses, workshops, corporate training programmes, certification courses, and consultancy services. This diversification helps stabilise revenue and mitigate risks.

4. *Partnerships and Collaborations:* Collaborating with industry partners, businesses, and educational institutions can enhance the credibility and reach of the Skill Acquisition Centre. Partnerships can lead to joint initiatives, guest lectures, internships, and job placement opportunities, further adding value to the centre's offerings.

5. *Brand Building:* Establishing a strong brand reputation for providing high-quality skill training can attract more students and create a loyal alumni network. Positive word-of-mouth referrals and testimonials from successful graduates can significantly boost enrollment numbers and revenue.

6. *Government Support and Incentives:* In many regions, governments provide support and incentives for skill development initiatives to address unemployment and promote economic growth. Taking advantage of these

government programmes can further enhance the profitability of the Skill Acquisition Centre.

7. *Continuous Improvement:* Investing in continuous improvement of course content, teaching methodologies, and infrastructure ensures that the Skill Acquisition Centre maintains its competitive edge and meets the evolving needs of students and industries.

Overall, with the right strategy, resources, and market understanding, establishing a Skill Acquisition Centre can be a highly profitable business venture in today's skill-driven economy.

70. ONLINE EDUCATION PLATFORM

Yes, an online education platform business can be a viable option for Nigeria's economy for several reasons:

1. *Accessibility:* Online education platforms can reach a wide audience across Nigeria, including those in remote areas with limited access to traditional educational institutions. This accessibility helps in democratising education and providing opportunities for people from diverse backgrounds to acquire knowledge and skills.
2. *Cost-effectiveness:* Online education platforms often offer courses at lower costs compared to traditional educational institutions. This affordability makes education more accessible to a larger segment of the population, including individuals who may not afford traditional tuition fees.
3. *Scalability:* Online education platforms have the advantage of scalability, allowing them to serve thousands of students simultaneously without significant infrastructure investments. This scalability enables rapid growth and expansion, catering to the increasing demand for quality education in Nigeria.

4. *Flexibility:* Online education offers flexibility in terms of scheduling and pace of learning, allowing students to balance their studies with work or other commitments. This flexibility is particularly valuable in a country like Nigeria, where many individuals juggle multiple responsibilities.

5. *Job Creation:* Establishing and operating an online education platform can create employment opportunities in various areas, such as content creation, instructional design, technical support, marketing, and administration. Job creation contributes to economic growth and reduces unemployment rates.

6. *Skills Development:* An online education platform can offer courses tailored to the needs of Nigeria's economy, focusing on skills relevant to local industries and job markets. By providing training in areas such as technology, entrepreneurship, healthcare, and agriculture, online platforms can contribute to human capital development and economic productivity.

7. *Global Reach:* Online education platforms have the potential to attract students not only from Nigeria but also from other countries, thereby generating revenue through international enrollments. This global reach can further strengthen Nigeria's position in the knowledge economy and promote cultural exchange and collaboration.

Overall, investing in an online education platform business can stimulate economic growth, improve access to education, and empower individuals to succeed in the digital age, making it a viable option for Nigeria's economy.

71. THE EDUCATIONAL CONSULTING BUSINESS

Educational consulting in Nigeria is flourishing due to the rising demand for quality education, personalised learning solutions, and guidance through complex educational systems. Young people with higher education should consider it a profitable venture because they can leverage their expertise to address these needs effectively. With their knowledge of modern pedagogy, technology, and educational trends, they can offer valuable services such as academic planning, admissions support, and educational technology integration. As the demand for educational consulting grows, so does the potential for young entrepreneurs to carve out a lucrative niche in this expanding market.

72. COMPUTER TRAINING INSTITUTE

In today's rapidly evolving world, technology plays a pivotal role in almost every aspect of life. Individuals, groups, corporate bodies, governments, and international communities are increasingly integrating technology into their daily activities to enhance productivity, efficiency, and innovation. Therefore, investing in establishing a Computer Training Institute is a strategic move for several reasons:

1. *Growing Demand for Tech Skills:* With the increasing reliance on technology, there is a high demand for individuals with strong computer and digital literacy skills. A Computer Training Institute can cater to this demand by offering courses that cover a wide range of topics, including programming, web development, cybersecurity, data analysis, and digital marketing.
2. *Job Market Opportunities:* As industries continue to digitise and automate processes, the demand for skilled tech

professionals is rising. By providing comprehensive training programmes, a Computer Training Institute can equip students with the necessary skills to excel in various tech-related careers, thus enhancing their employability and job market opportunities.

3. *Empowering Entrepreneurs:* Technology has democratised entrepreneurship by providing tools and platforms for individuals to start and grow businesses. A Computer Training Institute can empower aspiring entrepreneurs by offering courses on software development, digital entrepreneurship, and tech-based business skills, enabling them to launch and manage successful ventures in the digital economy.

4. *Addressing the Digital Divide:* Despite the widespread adoption of technology, there is still a significant digital divide, with many individuals lacking access to basic computer skills and resources. A Computer Training Institute can help bridge this gap by providing affordable and accessible training programmes to underserved communities, thereby promoting digital inclusion and empowerment.

5. Adapting to Technological Advancements: Technology evolves rapidly, leading to continuous updates and innovations in software, hardware, and digital tools. A Computer Training Institute must stay abreast of these developments and adapt its curriculum accordingly to ensure that students receive up-to-date training on the latest technologies and trends, thereby preparing them for the ever-changing demands of the digital world.

Overall, investing in establishing a Computer Training Institute not only addresses the current demand for tech skills but also positions individuals and communities to thrive in an increasingly digitalized and interconnected global landscape.

73. DAYCARE SERVICES

As civilisation progresses, societal norms have shifted, leading to more mothers joining the workforce in both the public and corporate sectors. With busy schedules and professional commitments, there is a growing demand for reliable daycare centres to provide childcare services for working parents. This trend highlights the crucial role that daycare centres play in modern society, and several factors contribute to the increasing need for such facilities.

Firstly, as more mothers pursue career opportunities, there is a greater demand for childcare solutions that offer a safe and nurturing environment for their children while they are at work. Daycare centres provide a structured setting where children can engage in educational activities, socialise with peers, and receive care from qualified professionals. This gives working parents peace of mind, knowing that their children are well cared for during the day.

Secondly, the rise of dual-income households has become commonplace in many societies, necessitating childcare arrangements that accommodate the busy schedules of both parents. Daycare centres offer flexible hours of operation, extended care options, and convenient locations, making it easier for working parents to balance their professional and family responsibilities without compromising on the quality of care provided to their children.

Furthermore, daycare centres play a vital role in supporting women's participation in the workforce by removing barriers to employment and career advancement. Access to reliable childcare enables mothers to pursue their professional aspirations, contribute to the economy, and achieve financial independence, ultimately fostering gender equality in the workplace and society at large.

Additionally, daycare centres contribute to early childhood development by providing enriching experiences and educational opportunities that promote cognitive, social, and emotional growth in young children. Through structured play, interactive learning activities, and individualised attention, daycare centres lay the foundation for future academic success and lifelong learning, preparing children for a smooth transition into formal schooling.

In conclusion, the increasing prevalence of working mothers in the public and corporate sectors underscores the importance of daycare centres as essential support systems for modern families. By offering reliable childcare services, promoting work-life balance, and facilitating early childhood development, daycare centres play a pivotal role in shaping society's future and empowering women to pursue their professional goals while nurturing the next generation.

74. CHILDREN'S ENTERTAINMENT CENTRE

Children from average or poor homes often lack access to the entertainment systems and experiences that their more affluent peers enjoy. This disparity underscores the significant opportunity for Children's Entertainment Centres to thrive as a powerful business venture for such communities. Here are several reasons why:

1. *Affordable Entertainment*: Children's Entertainment Centres can provide affordable, accessible entertainment options for families with limited financial resources. By offering reasonably priced admission fees or packages, these centres ensure that children from all socioeconomic backgrounds

can enjoy a variety of fun activities and experiences without breaking the bank.

2. *Inclusive Environment:* Children's Entertainment Centres create inclusive environments where children from diverse backgrounds can come together to play, learn, and socialise. Regardless of their economic status, children can interact and form friendships while engaging in interactive games, imaginative play areas, and educational activities, fostering a sense of belonging and community.

3. *Safe and Supervised Spaces:* For parents in average or poor households, safety and supervision are paramount concerns when seeking entertainment options for their children. Children's Entertainment Centres offer secure, monitored environments where parents can feel confident knowing that their children are safe while they explore and enjoy various attractions and activities.

4. *Educational Opportunities:* Many Children's Entertainment Centres incorporate educational elements into their offerings, providing children with opportunities to learn and develop new skills through play. From science exhibits and art workshops to interactive learning zones, these centres stimulate curiosity, creativity, and intellectual growth in children, regardless of their socioeconomic background.

5. *Family Outings:* Children's Entertainment Centres serve as ideal destinations for affordable family outings, allowing parents and children to spend quality time together without the financial strain associated with more expensive entertainment options. These centres offer a range of attractions and amenities that cater to different age groups and interests, ensuring that families can create lasting memories and bond over shared experiences.

6. *Community Impact:* By investing in Children's Entertainment Centres, entrepreneurs can make a positive impact on their communities by providing much-needed recreational and enrichment opportunities for children from average or poor homes. These centres contribute to the social and economic development of neighbourhoods by creating jobs, supporting local businesses, and fostering a sense of pride and cohesion among residents.

In conclusion, Children's Entertainment Centres represent a powerful business venture that serves the needs of children from average or poor homes. By offering affordable, inclusive, and enriching entertainment experiences, these centres play a vital role in enhancing the quality of life for families and communities, ensuring that all children have the opportunity to experience joy, excitement, and fun regardless of their socioeconomic circumstances.

75. SCHOOL SUPPLIES STORE

Starting a school supplies store indeed presents a promising business opportunity, especially for those situated in or around school environments. Here's why:

1. *Target Audience Proximity:* By situating the store near schools or in areas with high foot traffic from educators and students, you ensure easy accessibility for your target market. Convenience often translates to increased sales.
2. *Constant Demand:* Schools require a consistent supply of various items, from basic stationery like pens and notebooks to educational materials like textbooks and teaching aids. This ensures a steady demand throughout the academic year.

3. *Seasonal Peaks:* While demand remains steady, seasonal peaks, such as back-to-school periods, can significantly increase sales. Properly timed promotions and marketing efforts can capitalise on these peaks.

4. *Niche Opportunities*: Beyond basic supplies, there are niche markets to explore, such as eco-friendly or customisable school items. Understanding the unique needs of the community you serve can help you tailor your product offerings accordingly.

5. *B2B Opportunities:* Building relationships with schools can lead to bulk orders and ongoing contracts. This business-to-business aspect can provide a stable revenue stream alongside retail sales.

6. *Diversification:* In addition to traditional school supplies, you can diversify your offerings to include related products like educational toys, art supplies, or even school uniforms. This will widen your customer base and revenue streams.

7. *Online Presence:* While physical presence is crucial, establishing an online store can expand your reach beyond local customers. Offering delivery or click-and-collect options can attract busy educators and parents.

8. *Community Engagement:* Engaging with the local school community through sponsorships, events, or partnerships not only boosts brand visibility but also fosters goodwill, potentially leading to loyal customers.

9. *Adaptability:* The education sector evolves with technological advancements and changing curriculum requirements. Staying current with these changes and adapting your product offerings accordingly ensures relevance and competitiveness.

10. *Profit Margins:* While margins on individual items may be modest, the cumulative sales volume can generate significant profits. Additionally, bundling complementary items or offering value-added services can enhance margins.

In summary, a school supply store presents a promising business opportunity due to its proximity to the target audience, constant demand, seasonal peaks, niche opportunities, B2B potential, diversification possibilities, online presence benefits, community engagement advantages, adaptability requirements, and potential for profitable margins. Success lies in understanding and meeting the unique needs of the school community while maintaining flexibility and innovation in your business approach.

76. EDUCATIONAL TOY STORE

Educational toys are objects designed to stimulate learning and development in children while they play. These toys are intentionally crafted to promote specific skills or concepts, such as problem-solving, creativity, motor skills, language development, and social interaction. Unlike traditional toys, educational toys are designed with educational goals in mind and often incorporate elements of fun and engagement to facilitate learning.

In the Nigerian economy, the prospects for an educational toy store can be significant due to several factors:

1. *Growing Emphasis on Education:* There is a growing awareness and emphasis on the importance of education in Nigeria. Parents are increasingly recognising the value of providing their children with educational experiences from a young age, including through play.
2. *Rising Middle-Class Population:* With a rising middle-class population, disposable income among Nigerian families has increased. This translates to a greater capacity and

willingness to invest in their children's education and development, including purchasing educational toys.

3. *Urbanisation and Modernisation:* Urbanisation and modernisation have led to changes in lifestyle and consumer preferences. Urban parents are more likely to seek out educational toys to supplement their children's learning experiences and provide them with a competitive edge in an increasingly competitive academic environment.

4. *Demand for Quality Education:* Nigerian parents place a high value on education and are willing to invest in resources that support their children's academic success. Educational toys offer a hands-on, interactive approach to learning that complements formal education and helps reinforce classroom concepts.

5. *Supportive Government Policies:* Government policies aimed at improving the quality of education and promoting early childhood development can further bolster the demand for educational toys. Initiatives that encourage entrepreneurship and small business development can also create a conducive environment for starting and growing an educational toy store.

6. *Rise of E-commerce:* The increasing penetration of internet access and the rise of e-commerce platforms provide opportunities for reaching a wider customer base beyond traditional brick-and-mortar stores. An online presence can enable an educational toy store to reach customers in both urban and rural areas.

7. *Cultural Emphasis on Education:* Education is highly valued in Nigerian culture, and parents often prioritise their children's academic success. As a result, there is a cultural predisposition towards investing in educational resources, including toys that support learning and development.

Overall, an educational toy store in the Nigerian economy can tap into the growing demand for quality education, rising disposable incomes, changing consumer preferences, supportive government policies, the proliferation of e-commerce, and cultural attitudes towards education. By offering a range of high-quality, engaging educational toys, such a business has the potential to thrive and make a positive impact on children's learning and development across the country.

77. EVENT PLANNING AND MANAGEMENT

Event planning and management offer aspiring entrepreneurs a promising business opportunity characterised by its growing industry, diverse clientele, creativity, flexibility, networking opportunities, financial potential, adaptability to market trends, and personal fulfilment. With the increasing demand for professional event planners to organise corporate events, weddings, conferences, and social gatherings, entrepreneurs have the chance to showcase their creativity, organisational skills, and attention to detail. The flexibility of this business allows entrepreneurs to set their own schedules, work from home or establish a physical office, and specialise in specific niches or types of events. Building extensive networks of vendors, suppliers, and industry professionals is crucial for success, as it opens doors to new business opportunities and collaborations. While event planning can be challenging, the satisfaction of delivering exceptional experiences for clients and guests, coupled with the financial rewards, makes it a proper and rewarding business venture for aspiring entrepreneurs willing to put in the effort and dedication to succeed.

78. WEDDING PLANNING

"Saturdays are for weddings" is not just a popular slogan but a cultural phenomenon in Nigeria, highlighting the significance of weddings in the society. This cultural norm has turned wedding planning into a thriving business opportunity, often considered a gold mine for entrepreneurs. Here's why:

1. *Cultural Importance of Weddings:* Weddings are highly esteemed in Nigerian culture, symbolising union, celebration, and family unity. The cultural emphasis on weddings ensures a constant demand for professional wedding planning services.
2. *High Volume of Weddings:* Nigeria has a large population, and weddings are a frequent occurrence throughout the year, especially during peak wedding seasons. This high volume of weddings translates to a steady stream of potential clients for wedding planners.
3. *Elaborate Celebrations:* Nigerian weddings are known for their grandeur, lavishness, and attention to detail. From traditional ceremonies to elaborate receptions, there is a strong demand for skilled wedding planners who can orchestrate these events flawlessly.
4. *Rising Middle-Class Spending:* With a growing middle-class population and increasing disposable incomes, Nigerians are willing to invest significant resources in creating memorable wedding experiences. This presents lucrative opportunities for wedding planners to offer premium services and upscale packages.
5. *Diverse Cultural Traditions:* Nigeria is culturally diverse, with various ethnic groups, each having unique wedding traditions and customs. Wedding planners who understand and respect these cultural nuances can cater to a wide range of clientele and create personalised experiences that reflect the couple's heritage and preferences.

6. *Networking and Collaborations*: Successful wedding planners build extensive networks of vendors, venues, and service providers within the wedding industry. Collaborating with trusted partners ensures clients have access to quality resources and enhances their overall wedding planning experience.
7. *Emphasis on Professionalism:* As weddings become more elaborate and sophisticated, there is a growing demand for professional wedding planners who can deliver exceptional services with a high level of professionalism, organisation, and attention to detail.
8. *Social Media Influence:* The rise of social media has transformed the wedding industry, with couples seeking inspiration, ideas, and recommendations online. Wedding planners who leverage social media platforms to showcase their work, engage with potential clients, and build their brand presence can attract a larger clientele base.
9. *Personal Fulfilment:* Wedding planning is not just a business but a passion for many entrepreneurs who derive immense satisfaction from creating dream weddings and witnessing the joy of couples and their families on their special day.

In conclusion, the cultural significance of weddings in Nigeria, coupled with the rising demand for professional wedding planning services, makes wedding planning a lucrative and rewarding business venture. Entrepreneurs who understand market dynamics, embrace cultural diversity, prioritise professionalism, and harness the power of networking and social media can capitalise on the gold mine of opportunities within the wedding industry.

79. CORPORATE EVENT MANAGEMENT

Corporate event management indeed holds significant potential as a powerful business venture, given the corporate world's role as a platform for social engineering. Here's a comprehensive discussion of why it's a potent business opportunity:

1. *Strategic Networking Opportunities:* Corporate events serve as strategic platforms for networking and relationship-building among key stakeholders, including employees, clients, partners, investors, and industry peers. Event management companies can facilitate these connections through well-planned and executed events, enhancing business opportunities and partnerships.
2. *Brand Building and Image Enhancement:* Corporate events provide companies with opportunities to showcase their brand identity, values, and culture to a targeted audience. Event management firms play a crucial role in designing events that align with the company's objectives, effectively communicating its message, and enhancing its reputation in the market.
3. *Employee Engagement and Motivation:* Well-organised corporate events contribute to employee engagement, morale, and motivation by recognising achievements, fostering team spirit, and providing opportunities for professional development and networking. Event management companies can design tailored experiences that inspire and energise employees, leading to increased productivity and retention.
4. *Product Launches and Promotions:* Corporate events are often used as platforms for launching new products, services, or initiatives and promoting existing offerings. Event management firms can create immersive and memorable

experiences that generate excitement, drive sales, and enhance brand visibility in the marketplace.

5. *Thought Leadership and Knowledge Sharing:* Corporate events, such as conferences, seminars, and workshops, facilitate thought leadership and knowledge sharing within industries and sectors. Event management companies play a crucial role in curating content, securing expert speakers, and coordinating logistics to ensure the success of these events, positioning their clients as leaders in their respective fields.
6. *Crisis Management and Reputation Repair:* In times of crisis or reputation challenges, corporate events can be instrumental in rebuilding trust, restoring confidence, and repairing damaged relationships with stakeholders. Event management firms can collaborate with companies to plan and execute events that demonstrate transparency, accountability, and a commitment to positive change.
7. *Measurable ROI:* Effective event management involves careful planning, execution, and evaluation to ensure a measurable return on investment (ROI) for corporate clients. Event management companies employ data analytics, attendee feedback, and other metrics to assess the success of events and optimise future strategies accordingly, providing tangible value to their clients.
8. *Innovation and Creativity:* In a competitive business environment, companies are constantly seeking innovative and creative ways to differentiate themselves and stand out from the crowd. Event management firms leverage their creativity, industry expertise, and trend awareness to design unique and memorable experiences that leave a lasting impression on attendees and stakeholders.
9. *Adaptability to Virtual Platforms:* With the rise of virtual and hybrid events, event management companies have adapted

their services to cater to the evolving needs of the corporate world. By leveraging digital technologies and platforms, they can deliver engaging and interactive experiences that transcend geographical barriers and reach a wider audience.

In summary, corporate event management is a powerful business opportunity that leverages the corporate world's role as a platform for social engineering. By facilitating strategic networking, brand building, employee engagement, product promotion, thought leadership, crisis management, measurable ROI, innovation, and adaptability to virtual platforms, event management companies play a vital role in shaping the success and reputation of corporate clients in today's dynamic business landscape.

80. PARTY RENTALS

Party rentals indeed represent a valuable and lucrative business venture in Nigerian society, where social gatherings and celebrations are an integral part of the culture. Here's a comprehensive discussion of why party rentals are in high demand and present significant opportunities for entrepreneurs:

1. *Cultural Emphasis on Celebrations:* Nigeria is known for its vibrant and lively social culture, with celebrations such as weddings, birthdays, graduations, religious festivals, and cultural ceremonies being frequent occurrences. This cultural emphasis on celebrations creates a constant demand for party rental equipment and services.
2. *Weekend Celebrations*: Weekends are typically marked for various celebrations and events across Nigeria. From Friday night *owambes* to Sunday afternoon parties, there is a consistent need for rental spaces, chairs, tables, tents, decor, and other party essentials to accommodate guests and create memorable experiences.

3. *Growing Middle-Class Population:* With a growing middle-class population and increasing disposable incomes, Nigerians are increasingly willing to invest in hosting memorable and well-organised events. This translates to a higher demand for quality party rental services that can meet their needs and expectations.

4. *Urbanisation and Limited Space:* Urbanisation has led to a scarcity of space in major cities like Lagos, Abuja, and Port Harcourt, making it challenging for individuals and families to host large gatherings in their homes. As a result, they often turn to party rental companies to provide suitable venues and equipment for their events.

5. *Convenience and Cost-Effectiveness:* Renting party equipment and venues offers event organisers convenience and cost-effectiveness compared to purchasing or building these items. Party rental companies provide a wide range of options to suit different budgets and preferences, making it an attractive option for hosts.

6. *Diverse Offerings:* Party rental businesses offer a wide range of products and services, including tents, chairs, tables, linens, decorations, sound systems, lighting, catering equipment, and even transportation vehicles. This versatility allows entrepreneurs to cater to various types of events and clientele, expanding their market reach.

7. *Corporate Events and Functions:* In addition to private celebrations, there is a growing demand for party rentals for corporate events, conferences, seminars, product launches, and company retreats. Corporate clients often require specialised equipment and services, presenting additional revenue opportunities for party rental businesses.

8. *Event Planning Partnerships:* Party rental companies can establish partnerships with event planners, caterers,

decorators, and other vendors in the event industry to offer comprehensive solutions to their clients. Collaborating with these professionals enhances the overall event experience and increases customer satisfaction.

9. *Seasonal Opportunities:* Certain seasons and holidays, such as Christmas, Easter, New Year's Eve, and Independence Day, witness a surge in celebratory events and parties. Party rental businesses can capitalise on these seasonal opportunities by offering special packages, promotions, and themed decorations.

10. *Investment Potential:* Starting a party rental business requires relatively low startup costs compared to other ventures, as it primarily involves purchasing or leasing equipment and securing storage space. With careful planning, strategic marketing, and excellent customer service, entrepreneurs can quickly recoup their initial investment and achieve profitability.

In conclusion, party rentals represent a valuable business venture in Nigerian society due to the cultural emphasis on celebrations, weekend festivities, growing middle-class population, urbanisation, convenience, diverse offerings, corporate demand, event planning partnerships, seasonal opportunities, and investment potential. Entrepreneurs who enter this market with quality products, competitive pricing, exceptional customer service, and a keen understanding of local preferences and trends can establish successful and sustainable party rental businesses that cater to the diverse needs of their clientele.

81. PHOTOGRAPHY AND VIDEOGRAPHY SERVICES

Photography and videography services in Nigeria offer entrepreneurs a dynamic and lucrative business opportunity fuelled by the country's vibrant cultural landscape and the ever-growing demand for visual content. With celebrations and events deeply ingrained in Nigerian culture, from lavish weddings to corporate functions and cultural festivals, there is a consistent need for professional photographers and videographers to capture these moments. This presents entrepreneurs with a diverse range of opportunities to cater to various market segments, from individuals seeking personal event coverage to businesses in need of commercial branding and marketing materials.

Moreover, the proliferation of digital platforms and social media has heightened the demand for captivating visual content across industries. Businesses recognise the importance of visually engaging their audience and rely on photography and videography services to convey their brand message effectively. This translates into a steady stream of clients for entrepreneurs offering high-quality visuals that resonate with target audiences and drive engagement. With the accessibility of advanced equipment and editing tools, entrepreneurs can harness technology to deliver stunning visuals that meet the evolving demands of clients in the digital age.

Wedding ceremonies, in particular, present a significant growth opportunity for photography and videography businesses in Nigeria. Weddings are celebrated with great pomp and pageantry, creating a lucrative market for skilled professionals who can capture the essence of these elaborate ceremonies. Couples aspire to document their special day in exquisite detail, creating a demand for photographers and videographers who can deliver exceptional results. Entrepreneurs who specialise in wedding photography and videography can capitalise on this demand, offering tailored packages and personalised services to meet the unique needs of each couple.

Furthermore, entrepreneurship in photography and videography allows individuals to pursue their passion for visual storytelling while building a profitable business. Creativity and innovation are key drivers of success in this industry, as entrepreneurs strive to differentiate their services and stand out in a competitive market. By honing their craft, cultivating a strong brand identity, and leveraging marketing strategies to reach their target audience, entrepreneurs can establish thriving photography and videography businesses that contribute to Nigeria's vibrant cultural tapestry while generating substantial income and opportunities for growth.

82. DJ SERVICES

The DJ services business in Nigeria presents entrepreneurs with an exciting opportunity to tap into the country's vibrant music and entertainment culture. DJs play a crucial role in creating memorable experiences at various events, including weddings, parties, corporate functions, and cultural celebrations. With Nigeria's diverse music scene encompassing genres such as Afrobeats, Highlife, Hip Hop, and Afro-pop, there is a growing demand for skilled DJs who can curate playlists, mix tracks, and keep crowds entertained.

Entrepreneurs entering the DJ services business can capitalise on the country's bustling event industry, where celebrations are frequent and often extravagant. Nigerians love to party, and a plethora of social gatherings and nightlife events typically mark weekends. DJs play a central role in setting the mood, energising the crowd, and ensuring that guests have a memorable experience on the dance floor. By providing professional DJ services tailored to the unique preferences of each event, entrepreneurs can establish themselves as go-to entertainment providers and build a loyal client base.

Moreover, advancements in technology have democratised DJing, making it more accessible to aspiring entrepreneurs. With the availability of affordable DJ equipment, software, and online resources, individuals can pursue their passion for music and entertainment without the need for extensive capital investment. Additionally, social media platforms and digital marketing tools enable DJs to promote their services, showcase their skills, and connect with potential clients on a broader scale. By leveraging these technological tools and platforms, entrepreneurs can elevate their DJ services business, expand their reach, and capitalise on the growing demand for quality entertainment experiences in Nigeria's dynamic event landscape.

83. BALLOON DECORATIONS

Balloon decorations can be a lucrative business, especially for events like weddings, birthdays, corporate events, and other celebrations. Here are some key points regarding the prospects of a balloon decoration business:

1. *Growing Demand:* The demand for unique and creative decorations, including balloon art, is increasing as people seek more personalised and memorable event experiences.
2. *Profit Margins:* Balloon decorations can offer high-profit margins, especially for customised or themed designs that require skill and creativity.
3. *Low Start-up Costs:* Compared to many other businesses, starting a balloon decoration business typically requires a relatively low initial investment, making it accessible to new entrepreneurs.
4. *Seasonal Variation:* Business may experience seasonal fluctuations, with higher demand during certain times of

the year (e.g., holidays and wedding seasons) and slower periods at other times.

5. *Competition:* The market can be competitive, so offering unique designs, excellent customer service, and competitive pricing is crucial for success.
6. *Networking and Marketing:* Building a strong network with event planners, venues, and other related businesses, as well as effective marketing strategies, are key to attracting clients and growing the business.
7. *Regulations and Safety:* It's important to be aware of any regulations regarding balloon releases and to ensure that all decorations comply with safety standards.

Overall, with the right combination of creativity, business acumen, and customer service, a balloon decoration business can have promising prospects in the event industry.

84. CATERING EQUIPMENT RENTAL:

Catering equipment rental is a service that provides the necessary tools and items for events, parties, or functions where food and beverages are served. Here are some key points to consider:

1. *Types of Equipment:* Catering equipment includes a wide range of items such as serving dishes, cutlery, glassware, tableware, cooking equipment, refrigeration units, and more. The specific items needed depend on the type and scale of the event.
2. *Benefits for Customers:* Renting catering equipment is often more cost-effective than buying, especially for one-time events or occasions where specific items are needed. It also eliminates the need for storage and maintenance of the equipment.

3. *Business Model:* Catering equipment rental businesses can operate on a rental-only basis or offer additional services such as delivery, setup, and collection of the equipment. Some businesses may also provide staffing for events.
4. *Target Market:* The target market for catering equipment rental includes event planners, caterers, hotels, restaurants, and individuals hosting events such as weddings, parties, and corporate functions.
5. *Quality and Maintenance:* Rental companies must maintain high-quality equipment and ensure that it is clean, sanitised, and in good working condition before renting it out. Regular maintenance and inspections are essential.
6. *Logistics and Inventory Management:* Managing inventory and logistics is key to the success of a catering equipment rental business. This includes keeping track of available stock, scheduling deliveries and pickups, and ensuring timely and efficient service.
7. *Regulations and Compliance:* Rental businesses must comply with health and safety regulations regarding food handling and equipment sanitation. It's important to stay updated with local regulations and standards.

Overall, catering equipment rental can be a profitable business opportunity, especially in areas with a high demand for event services. Providing quality equipment, excellent customer service, and competitive pricing are essential for success in this industry.

85. EVENT SECURITY SERVICES

Event Security Services is a promising business venture in Nigeria. This business provides security solutions for various events, such as concerts, weddings, conferences, and festivals. It provides trained security personnel, crowd control, access control, and overall event safety management. With the increasing need for security due to various security challenges in the country, investing in Event Security Services can be a lucrative opportunity for entrepreneurs in Nigeria.

86. FLORAL ARRANGEMENT SERVICES

Floral Arrangement Services in Nigeria offer a great business opportunity for young entrepreneurs. With Nigeria's vibrant culture and the importance of celebrations, there is a high demand for floral decorations for events such as weddings, birthdays, funerals, and corporate events.

Starting a floral arrangement business requires creativity, good marketing skills, and an understanding of different floral designs and arrangements. Entrepreneurs can also explore online platforms to reach a wider audience and offer delivery services to expand their customer base. Overall, the Floral Arrangement Services business in Nigeria is lucrative and can be a rewarding venture for young Nigerians.

87. RIDE-SHARING SERVICES

Ride-sharing services in Nigeria involve the use of mobile apps to connect passengers with drivers who are willing to provide transportation services. These services offer a convenient and often more affordable alternative to traditional taxis.

In a country like Nigeria, where traffic congestion and transportation challenges are prevalent, ride-sharing services can significantly improve mobility and accessibility. They can also provide a source of income for drivers and create job opportunities for many.

For young entrepreneurs, starting a ride-sharing service can be a lucrative business opportunity. By leveraging technology, they can create platforms that streamline the process of matching passengers with drivers, ensuring a smooth and efficient service. However, challenges such as regulatory issues and competition exist, so entrepreneurs need to carefully plan and execute their business strategies to succeed in this market.

88. COURIER AND DELIVERY SERVICES

Courier and delivery services in Nigeria involve the transportation of goods and packages from one location to another. These services are essential for businesses and individuals who need to send or receive items quickly and reliably.

Despite the growing demand for courier and delivery services in Nigeria, there are still a limited number of companies operating in this sector. This presents a significant opportunity for more people to enter the market and establish successful courier businesses.

Entrepreneurs looking to start a courier and delivery service business in Nigeria need to consider factors such as logistics, fleet management, and customer service. By providing efficient and reliable delivery services, entrepreneurs can tap into a market that has great potential for growth and profitability.

89. CAR RENTAL.

Car rental is a service that allows individuals to rent vehicles for a short period, typically ranging from a few hours to a few weeks. This service is popular among travellers, business professionals, and individuals who need temporary transportation.

To own a car rental business, several steps need to be taken:

1. *Market Research:* Conduct thorough research to understand the demand for car rental services in your target area. Identify your target market and competition.
2. *Business Plan:* Develop a comprehensive business plan that outlines your goals, target market, pricing strategy, marketing plan, and financial projections.
3. *Legal Requirements:* Register your business, obtain the necessary licences and permits, and ensure compliance with local regulations and tax requirements.
4. Fleet Acquisition: Purchase or lease a fleet of vehicles that meets the needs of your target market. Consider factors such as vehicle size, fuel efficiency, and maintenance costs.
5. *Insurance:* Obtain insurance coverage for your vehicles to protect against accidents, theft, and other risks.
6. *Location:* Choose a convenient and accessible location for your car rental business. Consider factors such as parking space, visibility, and proximity to transportation hubs.
7. *Marketing:* Develop a marketing strategy to promote your car rental services. Utilise online and offline marketing channels to reach your target audience.
8. *Customer Service:* Provide excellent customer service to attract and retain customers. Ensure that your vehicles are well-maintained and clean.

Owning a car rental business can be a rewarding venture, but it requires careful planning, investment, and management to succeed.

90. LOGISTICS COMPANY

A logistics company is a business that manages the flow of goods and services from the point of origin to the point of consumption. This includes planning, implementing, and controlling the efficient and effective movement and storage of goods, services, and information.

Logistics companies are essential for entrepreneurs seeking to make money for several reasons:

1. *Growing Demand:* The demand for logistics services is increasing due to factors such as e-commerce growth, globalisation, and the need for efficient supply chain management.
2. *Diverse Opportunities:* Logistics companies can specialise in various services, including transportation, warehousing, inventory management, and freight forwarding, providing entrepreneurs with diverse opportunities to meet different market needs.
3. *Scalability*: Logistics businesses can be easily scaled up or down to meet changing market demands, making them flexible and adaptable to different business conditions.
4. *Profitability*: A well-managed logistics company can be highly profitable, as businesses are willing to pay for efficient and reliable logistics services to ensure the smooth operation of their supply chains.
5. *Innovation:* The logistics industry is constantly evolving, with new technologies and practices emerging to improve efficiency and reduce costs. This creates opportunities for innovative entrepreneurs to develop new solutions and services.

Overall, a logistics company can be an attractive business option for entrepreneurs looking to make money due to its growing demand, diverse opportunities, scalability, profitability, and potential for innovation.

91. FREIGHT FORWARDING

Freight forwarding is a crucial aspect of international trade, especially in import- and export-dependent economies like Nigeria. It involves coordinating and shipping goods from one place to another on behalf of importers or exporters. Freight forwarders are responsible for organising the transportation and logistics of goods, including arranging for storage, shipping, and delivery.

In Nigeria, where international trade plays a significant role in the economy, freight forwarding is a lucrative business opportunity. Freight forwarders help businesses navigate the complexities of international trade, including customs clearance, documentation, and compliance with regulations. They also leverage their expertise to ensure that goods are transported efficiently and cost-effectively.

Starting a freight forwarding business in Nigeria requires a deep understanding of the logistics and shipping industries, as well as strong relationships with carriers, customs officials, and other stakeholders. By providing reliable and efficient freight forwarding services, entrepreneurs can tap into the growing demand for logistics solutions and contribute to the country's import and export sector.

92. TAXI SERVICE

The taxi service business in Nigeria's transport sector is a valuable one due to several factors. With the country's growing population and urbanisation, there is a high demand for convenient and reliable transportation options. Taxi services provide a crucial link in the transportation network, offering on-demand transportation for individuals and businesses.

Entrepreneurs in the taxi service business can use technology to improve their services and reach a wider audience. By developing mobile apps and online platforms, taxi companies can make it easier for customers to book rides and track their drivers, which can lead to increased customer satisfaction and loyalty.

Additionally, the taxi service business can create job opportunities and contribute to the economy by providing income for drivers and other staff. Overall, the taxi service business in Nigeria is valuable for entrepreneurs looking to invest in the transport sector.

93. MOTORCYCLE BUSINESS *(Okada)*

The taxi business presents a significant opportunity for young people in Nigeria for several reasons:

1. *Low Entry Barrier:* Starting an okada business does not require a huge initial capital investment compared to other businesses. Young entrepreneurs can start with just one or a few motorcycles and gradually expand as their business grows.
2. *Flexibility*: The okada business offers flexibility in terms of working hours and operations. Young entrepreneurs can choose to work full-time or part-time, allowing them to pursue other interests or commitments.
3. *Growing Demand:* Nigeria's increasing population and urbanisation have created a growing demand for convenient and reliable transportation services. This creates a favourable market for okada businesses to thrive.
4. *Technological Advancements:* Technology has revolutionised the okada business, making it easier for young entrepreneurs to manage their operations. Mobile apps and online platforms

have made it easier for customers to book rides and for riders to navigate routes.

5. *Job Creation:* The okada business provides an opportunity for young entrepreneurs to create job opportunities for riders and other support staff, contributing to the economy and reducing unemployment.

Overall, the okada business is a viable opportunity for young people in Nigeria to start and grow a successful business while contributing to the development of the transportation sector.

94. DRIVING SCHOOL

Driving school is a lucrative business opportunity for young entrepreneurs in Nigeria. With the country's growing population and increasing number of vehicles on the road, there is a high demand for qualified drivers.

Starting a driving school requires obtaining the necessary permits and licences, hiring qualified driving instructors, and providing a safe and conducive learning environment.

Driving schools not only provide a valuable service by teaching people how to drive safely but also create job opportunities for driving instructors and support staff. Additionally, they contribute to road safety by ensuring that drivers are well-trained and knowledgeable about traffic laws.

Overall, driving school is a powerful business opportunity for young entrepreneurs in Nigeria. It offers a chance to make a positive impact on road safety while building a successful business.

95. MARINE TRANSPORT AND LOGISTICS

Indeed, marine transport and logistics is an area within the Blue Economy that is often underutilised despite its significant potential. Nigeria, with its extensive coastline and numerous ports, has a natural advantage for marine transport and logistics businesses. Here are some reasons why this sector is promising:

1. *Strategic Location:* Nigeria's location on the Gulf of Guinea makes it a strategic hub for maritime activities, serving as a gateway to the West African region. This provides opportunities for businesses involved in shipping, port operations, and related services.
2. *Rich Maritime Resources*: Nigeria's coastal waters are rich in marine resources, making them ideal for fishing and other marine activities. This abundance of resources can support a thriving maritime economy, including the transport of fish and other marine products.
3. *Growing Economy:* Nigeria's economy is one of the largest in Africa, with a growing population and increasing urbanisation. This growth drives demand for goods, which in turn increases the need for efficient transport and logistics services.
4. *Infrastructure Development:* The Nigerian government has been investing in infrastructure development, including ports and transportation networks, to enhance trade and economic growth. This creates opportunities for businesses in the maritime sector to expand and thrive.
5. *Job Creation:* The maritime sector has the potential to create a significant number of jobs, ranging from ship crew members to port workers and logistics professionals. This can help reduce unemployment and improve livelihoods, especially in coastal communities.

Overall, marine transport and logistics is a promising sector within the Blue Economy that has the potential to drive economic growth, create jobs, and enhance Nigeria's position as a maritime hub in the region.

96. WASTE MANAGEMENT SERVICES

Waste management services can indeed be a profitable business opportunity, especially in areas where there is a lack of proper waste management infrastructure. Here's how waste management services can generate profitable income for an entrepreneur:

1. *Collection Services:* One of the primary services in waste management is the collection of waste from homes, businesses, and public areas. Entrepreneurs can generate income by charging a fee for regular waste collection services. This can be done through subscription-based services or on a pay-per-use basis.
2. *Recycling and Processing:* Another profitable aspect of waste management is the recycling and processing of waste materials. Entrepreneurs can set up recycling facilities to process materials such as plastics, paper, glass, and metals. These materials can then be sold to manufacturers for reuse, generating income.
3. *Composting:* Organic waste, such as food scraps and yard waste, can be composted to produce nutrient-rich soil. Entrepreneurs can offer composting services to households and businesses, selling the composted soil as a natural fertilizer.
4. *Waste-to-Energy:* Some types of waste can be converted into energy through processes such as incineration or anaerobic digestion. Entrepreneurs can invest in waste-to-energy facilities to generate electricity or heat, which can be sold to the grid or to local businesses.

5. *Landfill Management:* While not the most sustainable option, landfill management can still be a profitable business. Entrepreneurs can operate landfill sites and charge fees for waste disposal.
6. *Consulting and Advisory Services*: Entrepreneurs with expertise in waste management can offer consulting and advisory services to businesses and governments looking to improve their waste management practices. This can include waste audits, recycling programme development, and regulatory compliance.

Overall, waste management services offer entrepreneurs a range of opportunities to generate profitable income while also contributing to environmental sustainability. By providing essential services and promoting responsible waste management practices, entrepreneurs in this sector can create a positive impact on their communities.

97. WOODWORKING AND RECYCLING OF SAWDUST

Woodworking and recycling of sawdust can be a lucrative business, especially in areas with a high demand for wood products and a need for sustainable waste management practices. Here's how these activities can generate income for an entrepreneur:

1. *Woodworking:* Using sawdust and other wood scraps, entrepreneurs can create a variety of wood products, such as furniture, flooring, decking, and decorative items. These products can be sold to consumers, businesses, and construction companies, generating income.
2. *Sawdust Briquettes:* Sawdust can be compressed into briquettes, which can be used as an alternative fuel source for heating and cooking. Entrepreneurs can sell sawdust briquettes to

households, restaurants, and industries, providing a cost-effective and eco-friendly fuel option.

3. *Animal Bedding:* Sawdust can also be used as animal bedding for livestock, poultry, and pets. Entrepreneurs can sell sawdust bedding to farms, pet stores, and animal shelters, providing a comfortable and absorbent bedding material.

4. *Composting:* Sawdust can be mixed with organic waste to create compost, which can be sold as a soil amendment for gardening and agriculture. Entrepreneurs can offer composting services or sell composted sawdust directly to consumers.

5. *Wood Pellets*: Sawdust can be compressed into wood pellets, which are used as a renewable energy source for heating and cooking. Entrepreneurs can produce and sell wood pellets to homeowners, businesses, and industries looking to reduce their carbon footprint.

6. *Crafts and Art:* Sawdust can be used in crafts and art projects as a filler material or as a component in making composite materials. Entrepreneurs can create and sell sawdust-based products to art enthusiasts and collectors.

By creatively utilising sawdust and other wood waste materials, entrepreneurs can not only generate income but also contribute to waste reduction and sustainable resource management. Proper planning, market research, and investment in equipment and technology are essential for a successful woodworking and sawdust recycling business.

98. BUILDING OF FIBREGLASS CANOES

Building fibreglass canoes can indeed be a lucrative business in coastal areas of Nigeria. Fibreglass canoes are known for their durability and longevity compared to traditional wooden canoes, making them an attractive option for fishermen, tour operators, and recreational users. Here's why this business has high prospects:

1. *Durability:* Fibreglass canoes are more resistant to water damage, rot, and pests compared to wooden canoes. This durability ensures that the canoes last longer, reducing the need for frequent repairs or replacements.
2. *Low Maintenance:* Fibreglass canoes require less maintenance than wooden canoes. They are easier to clean and maintain, which can be appealing to customers looking for a hassle-free boating experience.
3. *Customisation:* Fibreglass canoes can be easily customised in terms of size, shape, and design. This allows builders to cater to the specific needs and preferences of their customers, whether for fishing, recreation, or tourism purposes.
4. *Lightweight:* Fibreglass canoes are lighter than traditional wooden canoes, making them easier to transport and manoeuvre in the water. This can be advantageous for fishermen and tour operators who need to move their canoes frequently.
5. *Market Demand:* In coastal areas of Nigeria, where fishing and water-based tourism are common, there is a growing demand for durable and reliable watercraft. Fibreglass canoes can meet this demand and provide a viable alternative to traditional wooden canoes.
6. *Environmentally Friendly:* Fibreglass is more environmentally friendly than wood because it does not require cutting down trees for production. This aspect can appeal to environmentally conscious customers.

To succeed in the fibreglass canoe business, entrepreneurs should invest in quality materials, craftsmanship, and marketing efforts to attract customers. Providing excellent customer service and after-sales support can also help build a loyal customer base and drive business growth.

99. PORTABLE WATER SUPPLY BUSINESS

The provision of portable water in various forms, such as tanks, sachets, bottles, and kegs, can indeed be a fail-proof business in many areas of Africa where access to clean water is a significant challenge. This is one business you can hardly get wrong. Here's how intending entrepreneurs can make sustainable gains and return on investment in the portable water supply business:

1. *Quality Control:* Ensure that the water provided meets regulatory standards for potability. Regular testing and certification can build trust with customers and ensure compliance with health regulations.
2. *Distribution Network:* Establish a reliable distribution network to reach a wide customer base. This can include setting up distribution points, partnering with retailers, and using delivery services to reach customers in remote areas.
3. *Marketing and Branding:* Build a strong brand identity and marketing strategy to differentiate your water supply business from competitors. Highlighting the quality and reliability of your water can attract more customers.
4. *Diverse Product Offerings:* Offer a variety of packaging options to cater to different customer needs and preferences. This can include bottled water for convenience, sachets for affordability, and bulk water delivery for businesses and institutions.
5. *Efficient Operations:* Implement efficient production and distribution processes to minimise costs and maximise profits. This can involve investing in automated production

equipment, optimising delivery routes, and effectively managing inventory.

6. *Customer Service:* Provide excellent customer service to retain customers and attract new ones. This can include offering prompt delivery, addressing customer complaints promptly, and maintaining a consistent supply of water.

7. *Environmental Sustainability:* Consider the environmental impact of your business and take steps to minimise waste and promote sustainability. This can include using recyclable packaging and implementing water conservation measures in your operations.

By focusing on these key areas, intending entrepreneurs can make sustainable gains and achieve a positive return on investment in the portable water supply business. Providing clean and reliable water to communities can not only be profitable but also contribute to improving public health and well-being.

100. SUPPLY AND RETAILING OF GRANITE

Granites are a primary building material that is required for the commencement of every building and, as such, is a veritable source of business. In urban areas where large construction works are undertaken, the supply of granite to construction sites is a good business that can guarantee great returns. All that is required of a potential business person is to take a tour of all major construction sites and construction companies in town, have a discussion with them and establish good relationships with them. Then, go around every quarry and inquire about prices and logistics; meet truck owners or haulage companies to negotiate business with them and form a network. Once all this is done and a few supplies are secured, one can get business done even on the phone. All that is required is bank transfers, and you will begin to make good money.

On the retail part, there are so many people in local developing areas who are desperate to build but do not have the money to order a whole truckload of granite to start their building. Therefore, you offer these people the option of buying the granite in instalments by getting a site, dumping a truckload or more of granite, and splitting it into units to sell to the people. This is a business that I have been doing for close to a decade, and it is profitable.

Some advantages are that the product is not perishable, and the smaller the units you sell, the more money you make. You can sell using smaller trucks or even cement bags, etc. Note that the retail aspect is best for a newly developing environment.

Conclusion

As you wrap up this journey through 100 business templates, remember that the path to success is rarely simple. Each opportunity presents a unique set of challenges and rewards. What matters most is your willingness to learn, adapt, and persevere in the face of adversity.

This book contains a wealth of information and inspiration. Whether you are just getting started in business or looking for new opportunities, these ideas provide a road map to success.

Remember that the key to success is not just the idea but also your commitment to executing it.

About the Book

Often, intense and insightful discussions with great minds lead to the question of what business to start, especially for those who have money saved up from previous or current jobs.

This book, *100 Businesses Anyone Can Do To Make & Grow Wealth* is a follow-up book to another book titled *Becoming a Millionaire: Rules of Engagement for Beginners.* This became necessary because when a man's mind is made right and ready for action, he begins to ask questions. If a person acquires the right kind of financial education, a burning desire is created in him with some anger, and that boiling will result in a coordinated search for another set of information. The millionaire mind asks questions, and the answers from there will birth financial prosperity. Therefore, this book is a compendium of 100 business templates for a typical African economy. Informed, inquisitive, and financially intelligent minds could pursue and pick one or two ventures to engage in more wealth creation.

Career people from all walks of life could use this book to prepare for retirement from active jobs. In fact, those who are able to use the templates correctly might have the profitability of their ventures retire them from their current salary jobs. This book has answered the question of not knowing the exact business to start with.

ABOUT THE AUTHOR

Perelah Bebra Wisdom was born in Arogbo-Ijaw, Ese-odo Local Government, Ondo State. He had his primary and post-primary education in and around the creeks of Ondo State.

He has a Bachelor's degree and a Master's degree from Adeyemi College of Education, Ondo and Obafemi Awolowo University, ILE-IFE, Osun State.

He is a graduate member of the Nigerian Institute of Management (Chartered) and also holds a proficiency certificate in Management from the same institute.

He is an entrepreneur by practice and currently teaches entrepreneurship studies at the Olusegun Agagu University of Science and Technology, Centre for Diploma and Certificate Studies, Okitipupa, Ondo State.

Perelah Bebra Wisdom is the Managing director of Ayubabra Nigeria Limited and a member of an NGO's board of directors.

He is also a member of a special advisory board of a fast-growing news outfit in Ondo State.

He is a young man whose inspiration to acquire and teach financial literacy and advocacy for financial freedom was drawn from years of financial affliction due to a lack of financial aptitude.

www.ingramcontent.com/pod-product-compliance
Lightning Source LLC
LaVergne TN
LVHW041058150826
845673LV00007B/1825

* 9 7 8 9 7 8 7 6 5 0 6 8 4 *